THE NEW SCHOOL OF ECONOMICS

THE NEW SCHOOL
OF ECONOMICS

The Platform and Theory Behind
the New Physiocrats

Philip Allan

SHEPHEARD-WALWYN (PUBLISHERS) LTD

First published in 2018 by the author

Second Edition 2023
Shepheard-Walwyn (Publishers) Ltd
Parkway House, 107 Sheen Lane
London SW14 8LS
www.shepheardwalwyn.com
www.ethicaleconomics.org.uk

Second Edition with new Introduction and Prologue 2023
British Library Cataloguing in Publication Data
A catalogue record of this book
is available from the British Library

Paperback ISBN 978-0-85683-563-6
EBook ISBN 978-0-85683-564-3

Typeset by RefineCatch Ltd, Bungay, Suffolk
Printed and bound in the United Kingdom
by 4edge Limited

A Special Thanks

I would like to thank those who supported me during this journey and helped contribute to this book:

Tobin Shields, CPA, CA, CBV, and lecturer at the University of Waterloo
Dr. E. Naimbe, Editor
Kristina Dancheva, Illustrator
Gergana Georgieva, Chief Co-ordinator
Aneliya Kaleva, Advisor on Publication Printing
Usman Malik, Cybersecurity Advisor and Developer of our Web Platform
Kevin Silk, SEO Advisor
Dean Attali, Technology Policy Expert
Tom Bainbridge
Daniel McCarthy
Pepijn Schreurs
Serhat Altin
Darijo Miličević
Luis Ramirez
Antonio Gomez
Jeremy Laurent
Sergei Bryzhak
Marcin Nickiewicz

Table of Contents

Prologue: A Betrayal of Economics — The Unjust Fusion of Public and Private

At first glance, you may wonder what a book about some long-dead economists could have to do with the quality of your life. I want to reassure you that this book is designed to offer real, practical solutions to some of our biggest problems in our communities and our entire economies. At the heart of the book is a desire and coherent plan to help us to return "economics" to its original purpose.

Taken from two Greek words, our modern day "economics" refers to "oikos", meaning *home,* and "nomos", meaning *account* or *management.* At its very heart then, economics should strengthen our sense of belonging both to home but also to our communities. That it seems to do the exact opposite (and what we can do about that) is the focus of this book.

When you consider communities, have you ever wondered why some places in the world are full of life and activity, with busy outdoor markets, street food vendors, and lively public squares, while others appear lifeless and lack vibrancy? In a world where the cost of going out keeps rising, distances between people grow, and everyone seems to have less and less time, do you find it increasingly challenging to create new friendships? If public spaces allow us to exercise freedom of expression through words, then why can't we also express ourselves through commerce or cooking in these very same places? Why does it seem that neither left-wing nor right-wing politicians can ever agree on what should be in public hands and what should be in private hands, which leads us to the byzantine and contradictory rules & systems?

Further, why does it seem that nowadays, speculating on real estate is more lucrative than working a regular day job? Do you ever give that any thought? Would you be surprised to learn that this is deliberate? I say more profitable – that is until the market crashes and brings the rest of the economy down with it. Until the inevitable crash, our homes become money-making ventures and our focus, instead of making them and our towns vibrant places to live, a home becomes a way to make a fast buck because working for a living seems economically pointless by comparison.

As strange as it may sound, the questions I asked you above are actually all interconnected, and the answers to them lie in our collective forgetting of critical economic principles that were once widely understood. In the distant past, economists grasped the importance of properly defining and separating public and private, and in turn, land and capital - as far back as the Physiocrats (more on these in the first chapter), Adam Smith, the father of economics, and Henry George, a man whose work, in the 19th century outsold every book except the Bible.

In spite of their extraordinary usefulness, these foundational concepts of society and economics were obscured, and, suspiciously, land and capital were fused together in the field of economics as one singular factor of production. This strange decision to do so, hidden from public view, has led to a gross distortion of our economic system and has led to the myriad issues we face today. Even so, mainstream modern economists have periodically recognized this fact, and increasingly continue to do so. Economics juggernauts such as Milton Friedman on the right and Joseph Stiglitz on the left talked openly on the subject but stop short of suggesting coherent alternatives to the current system, as I do in this book.

So why is it so important to clearly define and separate public and private? If you don't have a logical philosophy behind them, we inadvertently create a web of restrictive regulations, such as zoning laws, that hinder the organic growth of housing, businesses, and other essential amenities. These restrictions not only fuel rising prices (due to constrained supply), but also stifle creativity, limit economic opportunities, and ultimately result in lifeless, monotonous environments. We draw nonsensical lines between what we're allowed to do and what we aren't, and what's taxed at one rate and what's taxed at another.

Similarly, the lack of clear differentiation between land and capital leads to an economic system that favors land speculation and consumption over productive business development. This perverse incentive structure discourages entrepreneurship, leaving people trapped in a cycle of chasing ever-increasing home values, rather than investing in activities that contribute to economic growth and social well-being.

The absence of a strong framework that defines what's in the public domain and what's private also undermines our freedom of commerce. Without clear protections for these freedoms, we find ourselves constrained by regulations that prevent us from establishing businesses within our homes, buying & selling goods and services where we see fit, or otherwise engaging in commerce that enriches our communities and fosters social interaction. For those who have travelled abroad, you might see hints that things elsewhere can work differently.

Furthermore, the high cost of living and the resulting financial pressures leave people with little time or energy to socialize, explore new hobbies (or explore in general), or even consider starting their own businesses. This further exacerbates the decline of our cities' vibrancy and our sense of community.

It's a travesty that land and capital, two distinct and fundamentally different economic components, have been carelessly, and perhaps maliciously, combined under the umbrella of capital. This amalgamation is not just a theoretical error, but an act that has had profound implications on our economy, society, and the way we understand and deal with economic issues.

In the past, economics clearly recognized the differences between land and capital. Economists understood that land, being a finite resource provided by nature, should be treated differently from capital, which is fabricated and can be produced through human effort. However, over time, corrupting agents within the field of economics began to fuse the two concepts, effectively obscuring the critical distinctions between them. By merging land and capital, they effectively hid the unique qualities of land—its fixed supply, its unique roles in production, and its ability to generate unearned income or economic rent—behind the more benign notion of capital. This deceit has allowed landowners and speculators (known as the 'rentier class') to accumulate vast wealth without contributing to the economy's productive capacity.

The consequences of this betrayal are far-reaching. Our current economic system is plagued by issues such as income inequality, housing affordability crises, and environmental degradation, all of which can be linked to the improper treatment of land as a form of capital. The fusion of land and capital has also contributed to the proliferation of rent-seeking behavior, as powerful entities manipulate the economic system for their own gain, exacerbating societal divisions and eroding trust in institutions.

It is imperative that we expose this deception and reinstate the rightful distinction between land and capital in our economic understanding. By doing so, we can begin to address the systemic issues that stem from this misrepresentation and work towards a more just economy.

The New Physiocratic platform, grounded in Georgist principles, offers a path forward to do just that, and to address these interconnected issues. By defining the relationships between public and private, and between land and capital, we can create a more just and efficient economic system that encourages entrepreneurship, fosters creativity, and revitalizes our urban environments.

Implementing the right policies and mechanisms to create a new economy can help us break free from the constraints of our current system, paving the way for more dynamic, affordable, and socially engaging lives. By embracing this new way of thinking, we can work towards transforming the nightmare we are living in into a dream of a brighter, more prosperous, and fulfilling future for all.

As we delve deeper into the New Physiocratic platform in this book, we will explore how new economic principles can help us regain control over our lives, our cities, and our economic system. By revisiting the knowledge that was once widely understood, we can identify the root causes of many of the issues we face today and implement innovative solutions that will reshape our societies for the better.

By embracing a shift away from some taxes in favor of others, we can create incentives for efficient land use, reduce speculative practices, and generate revenue for much-needed public infrastructure and services while lowering the tax burden altogether. Changes like these would alleviate some of the pressures on housing and commercial space, making it more affordable and accessible to all. By further shifting incentives away from consumption and towards production, we can enjoy even lower prices, better jobs, and greater economic security.

Additionally, by revisiting and redefining the relationship between land and capital, we can foster an environment that supports entrepreneurial spirit and innovation. This shift in focus will help create a more diverse and resilient economy, where individuals are rewarded for their hard work, ingenuity, and contribution to society.

But it's not just about distinguishing between what's public, what's private, or what's land, and what's capital. It's much bigger than that. You see, it's also about access, and access is all about freedom to produce, and in turn, the freedom to express through production. Just as land represents a monopoly over a specific location, denying access to it prevents us from living our freest and most fulfilling lives, since land is a vital factor of production, in addition to being an address at which we live. The same holds true for other areas of the modern economy that have become subject to excessive government regulation. Those overregulated areas become sectors to which we are denied access.

For example, how likely are you to secure a fair loan or investment in your business if regulations have raised the barriers to entry in the financial sector so high that only a handful of banks operate where you live? The same can be said for countless other overregulated sectors of the economy, including occupational licensing. While some rules and regulations must be revisited, others will inevitably remain, and for those sectors, we must ensure that people have the access they need in order to be productive. There exist ways to do so, but we first must become conscious of the situation. Our current economy stifles production and stifles productivity.

With ever-increasing taxes on productive output (personal income, business income) and regulations that encourage rent-seeking, combined with our flawed treatment of land, is it any surprise that productivity growth has stagnated? Just read on, and you'll see for yourself.

The time has come to create a production-centric economy, free from constraints to produce, and free from the taxes to produce - while ensuring that the public domain is shared and protected. We must separate what's public from what's private, to generate public revenue from public assets and provide private individuals with the access they need to be productive. We then need to empower ourselves to keep what we produce, without producers shouldering the entire burden of taxation. The time for change is now.

I'd like to offer you a roadmap for transforming our current economic nightmare into a dream of prosperity, fairness, and opportunity for all. By revisiting forgotten principles of economics and re-establishing the proper distinctions between public and private, and land and capital, we can create a more just and vibrant society, where everyone has the opportunity to thrive and find fulfilment.

The great news is that there is increasing interest in these simple, yet profound changes to our economic system. Whilst the current system may appear to be impenetrably strong, there has been a meaningful increase in interest in creating a fairer and more dynamic and entrepreneurial economic life for all of us. I begin this second edition of this book with the changes I have seen and then offer you a vision or dream of how we could structure our public spaces to transform our personal lives.

As with any community, its vibrancy rests almost entirely on our shared commitment and contribution to its success. So please do join us at www.newphysicrats.org. Just as your home, your street and your community would benefit from your active engagement, we would too. And the most rewarding thing is that you'll meet others committed to making a positive difference. Together, we have a chance.

Update & Reflection

Since the original release of *The New School of Economics* at the beginning of 2018, many of the points made would prove to be prophetic. A month after its release, Andrew Yang would publish his book advocating for some eerily similar ideas while achieving great notoriety in doing so, and ran for President of the United States on the platform soon after. The New School discussed the dangers of existing monetary policy in inflating asset bubbles and why they would be ineffective at increasing real investment without the fiscal incentives to do so. The book also discussed some of the dangers of the trade policy of the time, and the risks of focusing on consumption-led growth over production, which has since been vindicated with the increasingly difficult foreign policy environment and the application of sanctions. The book also foresaw a growing appetite to emphasize & safeguard culture and the impact that would have on world trade.

Finally, and perhaps most importantly, *The New School of Economics* predicted that rising fiscal deficits and inflation (despite being written during a time when deflation was still of concern in many places, and negative interest rate policies were in place) would force governments into a fiscal corner. I went on to write an article in September 2018 for *Progress.org* to elaborate on this point, called 'Why a Land Value Tax is Inevitable'.

By March 2022, a presidential candidate in South Korea would come within a hair of winning an election on a pro-LVT platform to alleviate housing unaffordability. Meanwhile, the pro-LVT communities would be a growing voice online.

With the reflection also comes recognizing that the book and its policy recommendations have room for improvement.

Since writing the book, I'd find myself adding to the long list of countries in which I've lived, moving to Asia in 2019 (where I remain), living through the COVID-19 crisis soon after, increasing global political polarization, and war in Europe. I also further developed my career in economic research, working on a project for an economic think tank in Thailand. Observing different approaches to these crises, all while observing the sources of economic (particularly in small business) dynamism in Asia and its exciting effects on culture, led me to place a greater importance on civil and economic liberties.

This translates to amendments to policy recommendations. Most of these would amount to a simplification of the platform. Scrapping the collection of income taxes and incentive levies on companies, this value could be more easily captured through the other taxes, and would adequately fund the dividend, income supplement, and sectoral banking system. Some of the regulations of the sectoral banks could be done away with as well, and it may also be possible for the public to capture some of the rents of money creation and seigniorage through the network of local credit unions. Whether the answer to a centralized system of credit creation is an array of digital currencies is unclear, however it is clear that the injustice of an oligopoly of financial institutions is of concern to an increasing number of people. Financial regulation has allowed institutions to maintain their monopolies by entrenching incumbents.

Post 2008, the evidence is becoming clearer that larger financial institutions favor lending to other large institutions, at the expense of new entrants. Those new entrants are even further constrained by regulation. The dizzying array of street vendors, small producers, logistical options, traditional food markets, and garage workshops, overlaying the large-scale mega firms and phenomenal infrastructure that I see here in Asia, produces an exciting and inspiring environment for commerce and culture (not to downplay the issues with oligopolies here). The New School of Economics has certainly addressed this to some extent, however, I would further emphasize the need for more decentralization, deregulation, localisation, and the ease for small players to enter the market. I'm enjoying having the option of eating unregulated, unpasteurized street food, and for my neighbors to operate a small workshop business from their garage.

The shift to a production-oriented, long-term oriented, decentralized economy with an expansion of economic and civil freedoms, and a limited, devolved government that receives its revenues from collecting rents instead of skimming productivity, remains a goal of the New

Physiocrats. Reflecting on this, I would suggest even more freedom for voucher-funded schools and even expand it to the institution of marriage, allowing private entities to create their own marriage contracts, and apply the private voucher system to other services that might be offered e.g. employment insurance. I cannot express enough the material improvements, vitality, and positivity that come from living under such a system, to such an extent that it solidified my views on liberty & choice.

Introduction

The Dream

Imagine a place of great beauty, where every detail — from the bench you sit on to the lamp that illuminates your street — is crafted with the essence, artistry, and finest materials of your region. How were societies able to afford such grand architecture hundreds of years ago, while today's cities are adorned with grey concrete and glass? Do you dream of going to work without commuting through traffic? Consider a place where space is abundant and used wisely — where you could enjoy the sights without worrying about car pile-ups, stop-and-go highways, and busy streets.

Good infrastructure always seems to be in short supply, and governments often have difficulty funding it. When it is built, the value of the land near the infrastructure rises in value, and its owners reap the benefits, but the rest of the community doesn't gain. In fact, it makes it more expensive and less accessible to you. Wouldn't you too like to benefit from these projects in some way? Do you wonder why your community can never seem to afford adequate infrastructure no matter how much the economy grows?

We allow space to be taken from us and monopolized. We no longer control our skylines or how our buildings look. Space is taken and used inefficiently. Land is not treated as precious, despite its scarcity. Is a single-storey parking lot the best use for prime real estate when it could accommodate more levels? How about vacant homes used by speculators, or held empty by banks; could those not be put to better use? Those who were lucky enough to be born in years past managed to monopolize space at a lower price; space that their children now cannot afford. Meanwhile, our tax dollars are being used to build infrastructure near other people's homes, while a few lucky homeowners benefit and see their property values soar. Those same people lose their incentives to work as they earn more from speculating on property.

Imagine being rewarded for your hard work, instead of having your income taxed away and often squandered by your government. If you work, and are contributing to your family and to society, why should you have to worry about your earnings; shouldn't you have ample to live, eat, and enjoy life? If you're struggling with low wages and high prices, does it make you feel underappreciated by your workplace and society at large? If you're a higher-income earner, who worked hard to achieve such a salary, is it not unfair that the government takes half your wages? Shouldn't your efforts be recognized?

And why, despite revolutionary communications technologies, are we wasting so much time each day on inconsequential tasks? Commuting to work, following trivial rules, and endless bureaucracy are monopolizing precious time. Why are our working hours growing longer while our national wealth and productivity grow with new technology? Finally, we ask why, despite our modern production techniques, are goods built to lower standards, with planned obsolescence?

We think it's time for something new.

Who are the New Physiocrats?

The New Physiocrats are a political-economic framework and certification body. We are a movement established on a new way of economic thinking, what we refer to as the "New School of Economics." We completely transcend left and right wing politics, and we are not a compromise between the two. We stand for natural fairness and justice, as opposed to artificially engineered outcomes that are imposed upon us. We support individuals doing what they enjoy, and what they do best; respecting individuality, not equity of outcomes. We ensure that individuals are fully compensated for their efforts. We believe in maintaining and promoting the cultures, traditions, and architecture of each region, so that the world has variety for us to enjoy.

We guarantee dramatically rising purchasing power for all citizens with our program, not only through the vagaries of good policy, but also through direct cash payments. With fascinating, innovative policies, we promise opportunities for all, not just a select few. We pledge to do so while simultaneously providing the absolute best environment for entrepreneurs and business, and while preserving and restoring our natural environment. We believe in eliminating waste and misuse of our physical space, so that we all have plenty to live in. We believe in maximizing our free leisure time, so that there is vastly more for everyone. We believe in long-term thinking, not strictly short-term decision making. And what's even more unique? We accomplish this through a series of automatic mechanisms that are built in to our new system, as opposed to tiresome bureaucracy and political squabbling.

This is not a platform that can be implemented piecemeal — it is a sum of its parts. Each piece of the platform machinery depends on another. Remove one, and the others stop. Implement them all, and a new, bright vision for the world, and for our lives, can begin.

The Decline of Current Market-based Models

Each economic school of thought over the past half-century failed to produce its stated outcomes. In periods before that, those that did achieve success proved they could not deliver sustainable results.

These goals included: providing a high standard of living for the entire population, eliminating poverty, full employment, complete capacity utilization, high growth rates, eliminating boom-bust cycles, efficient allocation of resources, and social cohesion. Policies implemented to achieve these outcomes at times produced positive results, but they were limited.

Mercantilism (the pursuit of trade surpluses above all else) stifled healthy competition, limited consumer choice, and resulted in imperial wars over resource acquisition. Marxism, in its various forms, requires no introduction. Severe misallocation of resources, a lack of incentives, and curtailed liberties sealed its fate in history. Asian corporatist economies, Anglo-Saxon market economies, and Nordic social democracies were arguably the most successful. However, even these models reached their limits, and their flaws were exposed. The Asian model suffered through bouts of serious resource misallocation and bad loans — hallmarks of state-directed growth. Japan was the poster child for these issues with its lost decades, and China eventually faced its own challenges. Anglo-Saxon economies struggled with stagnating median incomes, financial crises, widening inequality, and a loss of their national unity. A lack of national identity led to regional independence movements. The Nordic model invited the indolent, and those with sinister intentions, to take advantage of its generous welfare state, and left its hardest working contributors under a burden of painfully high taxes on their labor.

These market-based models (including the Asian, Anglo-Saxon, and Nordic variations), combined with increased global trade were all largely successful in creating wealth and innovation. They were typically combined with a degree of income redistribution, regulation, and purposeful market distortions, to varying degrees of success. There was a difficult balancing act; redistribution versus incentives for productivity, regulation versus innovation, free trade versus concerns over current account balances, and environmental/consumer/labor protection versus growth. There was no common ideology, direction, higher purpose, or unifying theme in these models — pragmatism was an advantage — but in most instances, it did create a high and rising standard of living for a large segment of the population. However, it eventually became apparent that there were limits to this progress.

None of the models successfully handled cyclical turndowns, or even periodic wrenching economic adjustments. Capacity, particularly labor, had rarely been fully utilized in most economies. Poverty, unemployment, and underemployment left many citizens suffering and without a sense of purpose. One of the oddities in some economies was an increase in total working hours despite rising productivity, in addition to low labor market participation, resulting in an unequal distribution of free leisure time. The majority of the models eventually either handicapped innovation and entrepreneurialism, or did not spread its benefits to a broad enough swath of the population to keep them placated.

The increase in world trade that had produced so much wealth and efficiency has benefitted many but passed many others by. In addition to the documented shifts in the labor market, global trade also turned the world's cultural mosaic into a monoculture, beyond what the globalization of media achieved on its own. Traditional cottage industry, artisanal crafts, and small-scale workshops were displaced by larger, more efficient, global operations. Although these outcomes were a net productivity gain to the economy, the dangerous rise in nationalist sentiment reminded us of the hidden cultural value of the traditional small-scale enterprise and traditional lifestyles, and what was being lost in the pursuit of economic growth. Enterprises that became too big to fail held economies hostage, not allowing for needed economic corrections.

Free trade *without* free movement of labor meant that people could not freely chase jobs that were relocated as a result of the trade policies.

Free trade *with* free movement left many people with a fear of losing their sense of national and regional identities. Specialization and comparative advantage were real, but they began to feel more like a narrower range of employment options in each domestic market. Meanwhile, those who were willing to follow their jobs abroad had their movement constrained by arduous work visa regimes. Resource-rich countries that experienced the benefits of specialization during high commodities prices, were later shocked by price swings, as their current accounts were perilously reliant on an increasingly narrow range of exports.

There was no question that the free trade model offered many benefits, efficiencies, and new opportunities. Low prices were a godsend for many, and savvy entrepreneurs found vast opportunities. However, eventually the increasing returns to scale reached their limits, competition reached its apex until export subsidies and distortions resulted in fewer competitors. Not all participants were playing by the same rules. At some point, people began to question what they sacrificed and what they received in return.

Polls understated the discontent of a forgotten underclass, concealed in labor force participation statistics that don't appear in headline unemployment figures. By the mid to late 2010s, a new breed of leaders emerged to collect their votes. These were leaders willing to use the heavy-handed measures that society demanded. People stopped believing in the benefits of restrained, indirect policies, became disillusioned with the old economic models, and were more willing to engage in policy experimentation. However, even these new leaders did not have a coherent model, ideology, or effective policy toolset to implement the desired changes. Moderates ruinously ignored the importance of culture and tradition leaving sinister, cunning politicians to address them. Some of the new leaders were reckless, and others channeled the public's discontent into darker, negative forces.

The most skilled and successful in society, those who were most needed to support any economic system, were bogged down by increasingly heavy income taxes. Their incentives to generate output eventually dwindled. Innovators became less innovative, productivity growth continued to slow, and as professionals found solace instead through passive investing and real estate speculation, the market no longer sought out essential data to allocate resources effectively. The talented class fled to seek employment elsewhere, along with overtaxed, overregulated businesses, which shifted their profits and operations offshore. No matter how low interest rates fell, new growth was harder to spur. The continuous monetary infusions by central banks were channeled into real estate more than ever before, and only resulted in asset price gains. Real-estate hoarding and speculation — while adding little societal value — became once again the road to personal wealth for many, while new home buyers were priced out of the market or saddled with increasingly large mortgages. Old habits would die hard, and lessons from the late-2000s crisis were quickly forgotten.

These challenges were the new reality, and this is why society cried out for a new school of economic thought. So without further ado: Welcome to the New School of Economics.

A digital rendering of how a new Nigerian capital city would appear under a New Physiocratic regime. Stay tuned and view our homepage (www.newphysiocrats.org) for variations of these renderings, to illustrate how cities would appear in other countries. Thanks to Kristina Dancheva for the illustration.

Part I: The Guiding Principles of the New School

The New School of Economics draws upon principles of nature, biology, and human society in its most natural state; forces that must be respected and channeled, not fought against. Learning from economic history, tradition, and the accumulated knowledge of the Stoics, Physiocrats, and Georgists, *The New School of Economics* rediscovers long-known principles that guide economies, human behavior, and aspirations. It then analyses modern economic history and our most recent crises, and uses these lessons to form a comprehensive platform to address economic, political, and social ills like no other platform can.

Although the Stoics (until the 3rd century BC), the Physiocrats (18th century), and the Georgists (19th century) all play leading roles in New Physiocratic philosophy, we see the original Physiocrats as our forefathers of policy. The word Physiocracy translates as "Government of Nature."

Many historical figures have observed the unique role that land (physical locations) plays in society and the economy, and how it can be utilized in policy to achieve justice. However, it was the original Physiocrats of 18th century France who developed the first comprehensive economic model, and it was a model which saw land at the core of production. Adam Smith later expanded on this in the *Wealth of Nations* by including land as one of the three factors of production; a factor later buried by more recent schools of economic thought. Henry George, the father of a movement now known as Georgism, contributed the most to spreading this message. While encompassing a diverse range of views, we consider these economists (who highlighted land as a factor of production) as an extension of the original Physiocrats. After being buried in the history books, *The New School of Economics* resurrects the key findings of the original Physiocrats, and builds on its observations. It is from them whom we derive our name, the New Physiocrats.

Out of movements such as Georgism (and the Physiocracy movement that preceded it) grew an economic platform from some of this knowledge, it has proven impractical for the modern world and never developed into a comprehensive ideology. This is despite how economists from both the left and right have wholeheartedly endorsed Georgist policies, in particular the land value tax. These movements defined space (specifically land) as a product of nature, and as something to be treated as the commons, while ignoring all other factors. As our knowledge grew, we discovered the relationship between space and time. As our societies evolved, our understanding of what comprised the natural commons changed. The demands of society changed as well. Yet these political movements did not. And because they didn't adapt to our modern conditions, they were long forgotten.

The New School of Economics expands on this old knowledge, modernizes it for the context of today's society and economy, and formulates a complete ideology inspired by nature and biological reality. The political manifestation of the New School is our organization: the New Physiocrats.

Under the program of the New Physiocrats, products of nature, which our labor never built or earned — summarized as time and space — must be treated as the commons, as should products of culture, health, and society. So too should products created by society itself, such as the legal system. However, earnings from human labor and creativity must be left in the hands of their creators. We earn what we create, and it should not be taken away from us. In fact, what we earn from our creations must be encouraged and magnified.

Since previous generations of economic models, we have learnt much about the unavoidable and beneficial behavior of nature, and of ourselves. We have observed the interplay between time and space. We have seen how species improve over time by allowing only the best traits to survive. We've observed how all the components of an ecosystem work together symbiotically to create a natural balance. Participants in an ecosystem all have completely different strengths, different interests and needs. Yet in nature, they are each using their position to the best of their advantage, and in doing so, strike a certain balance and harmony that keeps the ecosystem alive. It is a system based on merit; and merit is a core principle of the system we advocate. It is not always pretty, but it is an unavoidable force. It is also a force that can be channeled to the benefit of all. This is the lens through which the New Physiocrats view the economy, society, and government.

A market that operates more effectively than any in history; one which minimizes distortions, functions in accordance with these rules of nature, and allows each individual to pursue their strengths and interests, is a central element of this vision. However, an economy which achieves these aims has yet to be realized anywhere, and can only do so by applying the New Physiocratic principles in their entirety.

These concepts of nature must also apply to government. Today's democracies theoretically evolve in the same way as an ecosystem, or a market. When different needs arise from society, new parties can form, or new segments can form in existing parties, to capture the new voting blocs. The parties, which don't respond to these needs in time, die off. Yet in reality, democracies often fail to represent the interests of both individual segments of society, and the country as a whole. Byzantine political rules, gerrymandering, and corruption all work against the system. Furthermore, in democracies that are more representative of the populations they rule, the system can also work to the country's detriment. Conflicting interests in government either work against each other to get nothing accomplished, or favor interests with the loudest voices and the most lobbying power.

The New Physiocrats see countries and societies (and by extension their governments) like an ecosystem in itself. Each segment has its own conflicting requirements and interests, and its own strengths. Yet each has its own unique, irreplaceable function. Only by voicing the interests of each segment, reconciling their differences, and by having a mechanism in which to do so (within democratic framework), can the ecosystem progress as a whole. This mechanism is what makes the New Physiocrats' system of government different from the rest.

Finally, the New Physiocrats observe the empirical evidence from other countries and regions to decide on the most effective policies that are in line with the ideology and maximize positive outcomes. They also learn from the successes, failures, and crises of other countries and develop innovative, streamlined solutions to mitigate problems. The New Physiocrats have a deep respect for history and tradition, viewing it as a distillation of millennia of lessons; yet it does take them at face value, and views them analytically and with an open mind.

Our goals can be summarized as democratizing the products of nature and society, while maximizing the private ownership of the products of our labor. We define nature as both time and space, with space including not only land, but also visual space, air, and other products of the environment. We realized this was the first step to modernizing Physiocratic ideology, to create a generation of New Physiocrats.

This translates into a system that ensures our time and space are used effectively, to guarantee that everyone can easily afford a place to live, can enjoy the great beauty of our landscapes and architecture, have clean air to breathe, and maximize their free time; unimpeded by bureaucracy, commuting, lengthy legal battles, and long working days. Conversely, products of our own efforts, arc ours to keep. Although some dues are owed to the system that enables our efforts, our labor must be fully compensated.

It is impossible to predict where and when the next economic shock, or the next economic opportunity might arise. The New Physiocrats do not attempt to do the impossible task of prediction and planning. Instead, this platform, of The New Physiocrats, aims for preparedness and flexibility. It's a system that maximizes economic diversity and policy tools so that countries can deal with these changes as they emerge. It also employs automatic mechanisms, which provide individuals and business with their share of the nation's financial success, to amass large savings in the event of shock, and to better feel the rewards and consequences of their elected policies.

With these principles in mind, we envision a system where products of nature (such as land) are taxed, and where taxes on labor (income) are minimized, or even subsidized. It is also a system where we have a say in how our spaces (cities and landscapes) look, and where we have an abundance of free time to pursue our own interests and desires. We envision a system in which we see the results of sound economic policy immediately, through automatic cash transfer mechanisms, rather than waiting indefinitely for our efforts to bear fruit.

Georgism's Pragmatic Land Value Tax

Ahead of his time and able to see what few others could, Henry George had his own ideas to rid the economy and society of its ills. In 1879, George wrote what would be one of the most influential books of his generation: *Progress and Poverty*. It would not do justice to his writing to try to explain it in words other than his own. However, we will review

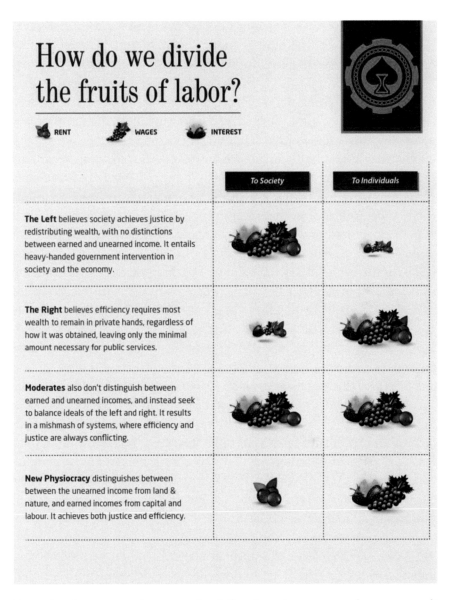

Rent, in the economic sense, is defined as income made as a result of special privilege (such as licenses, patents, and monopolies) granted over natural opportunities. This includes the monopolization of locations and land ownership.

the basic principles and how his policy prescription would work to resolve the ills of modern economic policy, and how it can be modernized to meet the needs of today's economy.

Henry George's followers were known as single-taxers, because they believed in eliminating all taxes except a tax on the value of unimproved land. This meant taxing the land itself, but not the buildings or crops upon it. This would have the effect of discouraging unused or underutilized land, without penalizing people for building or adding value to it. It would also force unused and underutilized housing supply onto the market. Both the left and right endorsed the land value tax (LVT). Economists from Adam Smith to Milton Friedman and Joseph Stiglitz recognized that the land value tax was the only tax that does not disincentivize economic activity, and can even encourage it. Unlike a property tax, which taxes the value of anything that is on the land (in addition to the land itself), an LVT does not penalize someone for improving the land, by building a house, a factory, or an office on it; only the underlying land it is taxed. Under an LVT, a plot of vacant land is taxed at the same rate as the land next to it that is being used productively (with a home, building, factory, farm, etc.) for its highest and best use. This penalizes the land speculator who is holding on to the vacant land, while not penalizing those who are using the land productively. The LVT encourages more land and housing supply, discourages speculators, and shares the wealth of the land with citizens. It is like fire under the feet of the landowners, encouraging the land's development. LVT drives down the cost of housing, and the entire burden of the tax is borne by the landowners, which allows labor and business to be relieved of taxation.

Unlike labor or capital, land cannot be moved, hidden, or transported to a tax haven. It cannot disappear if taxed; it cannot be hidden from tax authorities, and is therefore incredibly transparent. With a public land registry, it is simple to see who owns a given plot of land, its value, and the tax paid or due on it; tax evasion is nearly impossible.

Henry George also addressed the moral case for LVT. While labor and business activity is something we earn, land and its natural resources are inherited from nature. George argued that we are entitled to keep our wages from every hour worked because they are a product of our own labor. However, land is inherited from nature and is owned by whoever was first to arrive to it. The owner is then monopolizing that particular location, potentially keeping its use from those who can use it more productively. As the land is inherited from nature, it is therefore fair to tax it.

The combination of ethical and moral arguments wrapped up into one elegant solution made him immensely popular for a time. However, the Georgist movement never truly gained momentum. There were also questions about the feasibility of its implementation, and although it garnered support from both the left and right, there were no unified set of Georgist values to bring the movement together. The world changed a lot since George's era, but the Georgist movement did not.

More recently, economist Thomas Piketty famously analyzed the trends of wealth inequality, but failed to acknowledge the fact that land prices have been responsible for the majority of this trend. Instead, he advocated for wealth taxes, which are not only impossible to administer, but also don't address the root causes of inequality. He also failed to address some issues that are a matter of fairness, such as distinguishing between wealth gained through land price increases (wealth obtained from nature and the community) versus wealth gained through capital development (wealth obtained through labor). His proposal of a wealth tax was also riddled with feasibility issues, and was unfair and disincentivizing to those who create wealth with their own efforts.

Taiwan and Denmark, along with some states in the U.S., and Australia are a few places where the Georgist movement took hold for some time, and its policies were immensely successful, as seen in how these places have developed. Taiwan and Denmark still maintain strong, balanced economic development, with healthy current accounts. Some countries and municipalities still use an LVT with a great deal of success.

Although policy experts of all stripes frequently endorsed Georgist economic policy, without a modernized platform, without a flag, and without a leader like Henry George, sadly, the movement faded away, and its great ideas were quietly buried. Compounded by the interests of major landholders, and modern economists' tendency to censor the separation of land from capital, the ideas have struggled to return. In a world looking for answers to the big policy questions of our time, it is now up to the New Physiocrats to study, modernize, and implement these transformative ideas.

Modern-Day Examples

The New Physiocrats look to modern-day Taiwan and Estonia as national examples that have successfully implemented some of the New Physiocratic ideas and policies. Sun Yat-sen, the founder of modern-day Taiwan, was an ardent Georgist, and his successor governments implemented Georgist and other Physiocratic policies.

Since its independence from the USSR, Estonia has pursued a less ideological and more technocratic path to its development, but with many of the same policies and results. Both countries have used a land value tax. Taiwan became one of the most prosperous places on earth, and Estonia has been among the fastest post-communist countries to catch up with its developed peers, with the world's most successful and innovative governing methods. While the New Physiocratic ideas grew independently, we saw that we were not the only ones to want to implement these ideas.

The New Physiocratic Platform

The platform of the New Physiocrats (outlined in detail at the end of this book), includes economic, social, and political policy reforms. It includes a shift away from taxes on earned incomes, to the point where labor, savings, and investment are effectively subsidized with direct cash transfers. Taxation is instead shifted onto unearned income, in particular by capturing increases in land value and environmental use. Physical space and time are democratized in this platform, resulting in regaining control of our architecture, natural environment, landscapes, and leisure time. It includes innovative measures to minimize economic distortions and information asymmetry, and to maximize economic diversity and employment opportunities. New Physiocratic social policies tackle difficult demographic, cultural, and family issues, while simultaneously maximizing freedom of expression and natural liberties. The political reforms include creating an outlet for every economic and social facet of a country to voice their desires in a transparent manner, while reconciling their interests in a way to work towards the public's long term goals.

Our Flag

The flag of the New Physiocrats captures the tenets outlined in this manifesto and the party platform.

The core of the flag consists of land (illustrated with a spade in its center), integrated with an hourglass. This represents the public recapture of our time and space, in essence, an expansion of Georgism, which focused primarily on space. The fusion of time and space as spacetime [in the realm of physics] became more widely discussed a bit later than Henry George's publication of *Progress and Poverty*. The transparency of the hourglass in the center makes a statement of transparency [in governance] at our core.

The recognizable spade symbol, as a bettor might see in a deck of cards, also serves as positive recognition for the risk-taking nature of the entrepreneurs.

Combining the chain of DNA/cellular division with the gear, represents industry powered by our biology, and an encompassment of the flexible, evolutionary quality of nature. This alludes to Physiocracy's respect for nature itself, natural laws, the beauty of biological differences with the specializations it creates, and the organic nature of a functioning market economy. In essence, harnessing the power of human behavior and market economics to drive national industry.

Eight teeth in a gear, with eight notches, represent the 16 economic goals represented by the Sectoral Banks, of different weighting in governing influence. The three rings (from the inside moving out), represent the original factors of production: land, labor, and capital. Land is represented by the sandy ring encircling the spade, the DNA/dividing cells representing human labor, and the gear representing capital. The shape of the four-layered symbol in its entirety mirrors the shape of the proposed national parliament, with its four chambers.

The colors, brown with blue, were intended to represent land, air, and water. These are the elements of the earth that Physiocrats consider to have a public dimension, not created by human labor, and suitable for taxation.

These particular shades of the colors were used to create a feeling of majesty and tradition. Tradition, while not always a suitable advisor for the modern world, is a domain that the New Physiocrats appreciate as

Flag created with the help of Reddit's "youtytoo" and professional artist, Kristina Dancheva for the final version.

something to be considered (along with laws of nature), as a distillation of many years of lessons learned from history.

The respect of both science and tradition, new and old, urban and rural, symbolizes a reconciliation of two warring sides of the political spectrum.

Part II: Economic Reform Platform

The Three Pillars of Income Security

The Three Pillars are the backbone of the New Physiocrats' plan for providing economic support for the population, intended to replace the minimum wage and a host of complex social programs that exist today. In conjunction with the rest of the platform, it would ensure an economy at full employment, maximum incomes, and the greatest possible purchasing power.

- National Dividend (ND) — provided to all adult citizen-residents
- National Income Supplement (NIS) — provided to all those in the labor market, plus homemakers
- Assisted Savings Program (ASP) — a mechanism to magnify savings and pension investments

There must be three pillars of income security in a New Physiocratic regime. The first is the National Dividend, comprised of revenues gained from levies on common property (except land, the revenues of which go to fund general expenditures). The second pillar is the National Income Supplement; mainly comprised income tax revenues in their entirety (in addition to some other sources, to underwrite labor costs). The final pillar is the Assisted Savings Program, where savings and investments are topped up from capital gains taxes and small financial levies, such as those on short-term capital inflows.

Paystubs under the New Physiocrats would look like this for an average-, low- and high-income workers:

Average Income Earner

Your Employer	Company X			Monthly Salary		
Your Name		Your ID Number	Pay Period		Pay Date	
Average Income Earner		123456XYZ	01-01 - 31-01		31-01-XXXX	
		Hourly Rate	Hours Worked / Week		Hours Worked	Gross Salary
		25	30		120	3,000

Gross Salary		3,000				
Tax	8%	-240				
National Income Supplement	Full	750				
National Dividend		125	Pension Contribution	5%	182	
Net Salary		3,635	ASP Benefit		80	
Pension Contribution		-182				
Deposit in Your Bank Account		3,453				
Deposit in Your ASP Account		262				
Total Pay		3,715				

Low Income Earner

Your Employer	Company X			Monthly Salary		
Your Name		Your ID Number	Pay Period		Pay Date	
Low Income Earner		123456XYZ	01-01 - 31-01		31-01-XXXX	
		Hourly Rate	Hours Worked / Week		Hours Worked	Gross Salary
		25	15		60	1,500

Gross Salary		1,500	Pension Contribution	5%	94	
Tax	8%	-120	ASP Benefit		40	
National Income Supplement	Partial	375				
National Dividend		125				
Net Salary		1,880				
Pension Contribution		-94				
Deposit in Your Bank Account		1,786				
Deposit in Your ASP Account		134				
Total Pay		1,920				

High Income Earner

Your Employer	Company X			Monthly Salary		
Your Name		Your ID Number	Pay Period		Pay Date	
High Income Earner		123456XYZ	01-01 - 31-01		31-01-XXXX	
		Hourly Rate	Hours Worked / Week		Hours Worked	Gross Salary
		125	30		120	15,000

Gross Salary		15000	Pension Contribution	10%	1,374	
Tax	5,833 @ 8%	-467	ASP Benefit		160	
	6,667 @ 16%	-1,067				
	2,500 @ 24%	-600				
National Income Supplement	Full	750				
National Dividend		125				
Net Salary		13,741				
Pension Contribution		-1,374				
Deposit in Your Bank Account		12,367				
Deposit in Your ASP Account		1,534				
Total Pay		13,901				

The paystubs of average-, low-, and high-income earners under a New Physiocratic administration. The National Dividend (ND) amount is paid in full to all citizen-residents, regardless of employment status. The National Income Supplement (NIS) amount would be paid in full for those earning average incomes or higher, and prorated for those earning less. The Assisted Savings Program amount is paid based on contribution amounts, up to a maximum value based on median income.

Estimated values are based on Canadian, U.S., and U.K. tax revenues and incomes.

Under the Three Pillars program, lower and middle class income earners pay a steeply negative net rate of income tax, while high-income earners would pay a rate that approaches zero. Meanwhile, relative living expenses under the New Physiocrats' regime would fall considerably, the reasons for which are discussed later.

As with the other Three Pillars, the National Dividend payment would vary from month to month, as the value is based on the revenues raised. However, it would be offered to everyone regardless of employment status, and it would provide stability and bargaining power for workers. The National Income Supplement would supercharge earnings for those in the labor market (replacing the minimum wage and collective bargaining), encourage entry into the workforce, and effectively subsidize wages for employers. The Assisted Savings Program would amplify citizens' savings and pensions, replacing bankrupt state pension systems. All of the Three Pillars would be direct cash transfers, without the need for deficits or excess bureaucracy. This is only possible with general government revenues relying on the Unified Location Tax and Sustainable Value Added Tax, which are discussed below. However, the Three Pillars and other New Physiocratic programs would eliminate the need for some of the current governments' largest expenditures, such as state pensions, unemployment benefits, and other social programs.

Commons Levies for the National Dividend

Radio spectrum, big data, use of airspace and waterways, courts, monopolies, and unused patents hold a special place in the New Physiocratic platform. As they are products of nature or society, the special annual levies raised from these sources must be distributed as cash payments as part of the National Dividend. Examples of levies to be charged on certain common natural assets would be as follows:

- Yearly license fees for using radio and other public spectrum
- Surtax on monopoly profits
- Annual levies on "Big Data" companies' (e.g., Facebook) ad revenues, who use your information to their benefit
- Annual levies on unused patents (after a certain amount of time) / "patent troll" behavior

- Tax on settlements from litigation in court, paid by those losing the case
- Tax on air and waterway traffic

Hotels and similar entities (e.g., Airbnbs) must levy the Sustainable Value Added Tax at the luxury tax rate, as a consumption tax whose revenues also go toward the National Dividend. The growth of global tourism has brought many benefits to select segments of society, it has come at a great cost. Its effect on local cultures and way of life, traffic, and its role in driving up housing costs has caused tremendous pushback from communities around the world. Some communities, especially in Europe, have responded with hard caps on tourist numbers. However, these caps are also detrimental (and arbitrary) not to mention it is very difficult to control the flow of people. By channeling the powerful forces of tourism to enhance the national dividend, the revenues of tourism can be enjoyed by everyone, while at the same time, slowing its growth. As culture and space are considered public domain under a New Physiocratic regime, this is the most just approach to mitigating the impacts of tourism.

Lessons Learned and Property Bubbles

Crisis after crisis, economies and governments seem destined to make the same mistakes repeatedly. We let property (land) prices rise as interest rates decline, as we direct a disproportionate amount of credit into the real estate market. A large percentage of consumer spending, capital gains, and employment then becomes tied to land prices, as does the health of banks (and by extension, the financial sector). Once prices inevitably drop, the effects reverberate throughout the broader economy. Property markets in many Western countries are already due for a dip in 2019, and a more painful downturn in the mid-to-late 2020s, according to Georgist land value cycle theories. Credit is repeatedly wasted on land speculation instead of improving productive capacity, and the economy suffers as a result.

Incentives also become immensely skewed with rising land prices. During upswings, income from property speculation tends to increase at a faster rate than income from labor. It becomes more profitable to flip houses than to earn income through meaningful employment. Property no longer means a place to live, but has instead become a means to speculate in an attempt to accumulate wealth in the face of stagnating wages and dwindling pensions. Governments accentuate the issue by taking taxes from incomes, and using them to fund infrastructure, which further drives up the value of the landholders' properties at the expense of income. Some governments further compound the issue with mortgage income tax deductions, and lax rules on minimum home deposits.

Land value is a function of the size, location, and traits of the land. The land value tax (LVT) promotes efficient use of land by discouraging vacant lots, and because tax rates don't rise as the owners add value to the land, it encourages land owners to build upward. However, just as high land prices close to the city center encourage building/living away from the center, an LVT (which reflects those prices) would do the same.

The LVT, in its known form, has numerous shortcomings:

- Inadequately addresses urban sprawl, by encouraging building in places of lower land value
- Encourages speedy construction, which can lead to low quality structures
- Encourages rapid depletion of resources
- Doesn't address architectural standards (their design, cultural and environmental impact)
- Punishes sectors that require space (e.g., agriculture, some industries) to take advantage of scale
- Doesn't acknowledge private contribution to community land value, by taxing its entirety
- Is best used for infrastructure/government funding rather than minimum income / income supplement schemes
- Taxes businesses that do not yet generate profits (nor revenues)

Why do we want dense cities rather than sprawling ones? Dense cities have the following characteristics:

- Rationalized use of precious space
- Reduced transportation / commute times
- Reduced urban infrastructure costs (shorter metro lines, etc.)
- Rapid dispersal of ideas
- Higher levels of productivity

Unified Location Tax (ULT)

A Unified Location Tax (ULT) would include a land size tax which multiplies land value by plot size, to give size extra weighting. For example, it would comprise of an annual land value tax of 3% of the land's value, plus an additional 1% tax which multiplies land value by size. This would minimize urban sprawl, the use of space and materials, and condense the cities. Small-area, high-rise properties in the city would be fairly unaffected (small plot size), as would large plots of land in the countryside (low market value). Instead, it would target urban / suburban sprawl on the outskirts of the city. With large volumes of housing supply forced back onto the market, and no more vacant lots for speculators, it becomes much more affordable to live in the center, with far more availability. In addition, it would include taxes on the built structure if particular environmental, social, or architectural guidelines were not met.

We see the ULT as a means of development like an artist creating clay pottery. The taxes on *land* would act as a pottery wheel, providing upward pressure, forcing clay upwards from the base. Conditional taxes on *buildings* would act as the artist's hands, putting downward pressure on the clay, moulding it into the desired forms.

As land taxes throw fire under the feet of land owners, encouraging them to build, develop, and utilize the land rapidly, a ULT would address the following needs:

- Enterprises that require large spaces to achieve economies of scale cannot be unfairly penalized
- Buildings must be created with safety in mind, and not solely with rapid construction
- A large and growing stock of affordable housing must be incentivized
- Relevant architecture that is agreed upon by democratic process within each governing region
- Outlets that ensure ample supply and low prices for essential consumer goods
- Construction that safeguards the environment
- Land owners are rewarded for their property's contribution to the community
- Equal opportunity to afford land and its ULT rates

By allowing a certain number of deductions against the ULT for particular agricultural, industrial, and construction inputs and outputs (e.g., up to half of the ULT bill), as well as the wholesale purchase of Basic Essentials, it can ensure the survival of agricultural and industrial operations that benefit from increasing returns to scale. This would effectively be a double deduction (as these expenses would also be deducted from corporate profits). It would ensure that building construction is not rushed (as a matter of safety), and would reward the use of more appealing architecture and materials. Of course, to ensure that tax revenue is generated and to ensure the societal benefits of a ULT is maintained, there would need to be a ceiling for the maximum amount of deductions (as suggested, up to half the ULT amount). Unlike income taxation, it would be much more difficult to abuse deductions on land taxes. As the land registry is made public, the land's purpose, owner, and all details of its tax payments should be public at the registry as well. Because land cannot be hidden, it would be difficult to hide false claims from the public. If land is held for speculative purposes with no activity on it, the public and media would have the ability to investigate.

The ULT would encourage affordable housing and shopping, as well as land that is only host to buildings that meet the nationally/locally defined architectural and environmental codes (higher levels of water runoff with no collection, no solar panels nor green roof, etc.). This would be done through a higher tax rate on properties which do not meet these criteria. This would effectively compensate citizens for the use of the natural environment, without penalizing development, while simultaneously boosting the supply (and therefore affordability) of basic goods and affordable housing. The ULT would include a small tax on properties that don't meet these requirements, as well as on land with no activity. The building tax would need to be implemented more like a property tax, including both the value of the building and the land under it. This is because an ugly building or a smoke-belching factory in a well-trafficked area would have a much more negative impact on more people in a high-value (high-traffic) area versus a low-value one. Such a policy may allow for the elimination, or at least simplification of, onerous zoning laws, which tend to be an avenue for corruption and restrained housing supplies.

The only area where a ULT might need to be exempted or modified, is in the area of oil and mineral extraction, where it might encourage a more rapid depletion of the said resources. Instead, a separate tax regime must be implemented specifically for the resource sector, where rates are predictable and transparent, and rise and fall in response to price changes. The tax revenues from these sectors would be shared between the Three Pillars, a national sovereign wealth fund, and the Sectoral Banks. Because one of the Sectoral Banks is the Resource Exploration Bank, some of these funds would return to the resource sector anyway, while simultaneously stimulating diversification in other areas — potentiating these forces during resource booms.

The following is the recommended method for a first ULT implementation attempt:

Land Taxes:
3.0% – Land Value Tax (on the unimproved value of land, not on improvements nor properties)
1.0% – Land Size Tax (land value multiplied by the size of the plot)
1.5% – Additional land value tax on land for plots that are vacant or not in use at all

Building Taxes:
   0.5% – Tax on buildings (based on area and property value) not meeting national/regional architectural standards
   0.0- 0.5% – Tax on buildings based on environmental/water impact of the building
   0 .0- 0.5% – Tax on buildings based on how much of the building is used for essential living purposes (affordable housing, basic goods)

In total, a ULT consists of: a land value tax, a land size tax, a vacant land tax, and building taxes that are only applied based on social, environmental, visual impacts. It would be combined with deductions based on agricultural and industrial inputs and outputs, and wholesale purchases of basic goods. Affordable housing (defined by its price-per-square meter as a percentage of median income), for example would be exempt from the property tax portion of the ULT, moulding cities' skylines to contain more of these units.

If up to half the land taxes could be deducted for these special inputs, the tax on land would effectively range between 2.0 and 5.5%. The building taxes would not be applied at all if the guidelines are met.

This would add a tremendous amount of upward pressure to build, while ensuring basic needs are met for the population. It also ensures their visual space is preserved, without impeding business or creative freedoms.

All properties would have a publicly visible plaque from the tax authority with a QR code, to retrieve information about its certificates, property size, purpose, land value, building value, and the tax rate being paid for the property. This would be linked with the current data in the land registry, and would ensure transparency. For example, if you walked past an office building that you thought might be a good location for living, you could see if it was paying the appropriate tax rate based on the criteria. If it was supposed to have affordable housing units, you would then be able to verify this, as the land registry information would also include a list of residents with the contact information they volunteer, along with a list of available (or soon-to-be available) units. If tax fraud was suspected, this could be reported to an independent investigatory agency.

A ULT, defined by these requirements, would maximize the benefits of land value taxation, while minimizing its faults. It would in fact be even more mindful of Henry George's principle that physical locations are something we inherit from nature, by ensuring land would be purposed for the needs of the population, and providing an abundance of affordable housing and food supplies, all without wasted space. While an LVT as George envisioned would distort the economy away from agriculture and manufacturing due to these sectors' spatial requirements, a ULT seeks to eliminate this distortion. Meanwhile, a ULT further treats locations as the commons, by giving the community a say in their appearance, skyline, and architectural style, while discouraging negative environmental externalities. By using taxation as opposed to regulation to achieve these means, it preserves personal choice and allows businesses to progress and make appropriate decisions regarding their land use, instead of being bogged down in lengthy approval processes and uncertainties.

As Henry George noted, one of the great advantages of land/location taxes (the ULT in this case), is that the value of land increases disproportionately to the value of infrastructure built on it, which makes infrastructure projects self-funding. For example, if a new metro line is built in a particular location, the value of that land would rise dramatically. The lower the usage fee for this metro line, the more valuable the land around it would be. (What citizen wouldn't want to live next to a metro line that's inexpensive or free to ride?) By capturing this increase in value resulting from infrastructure development through a ULT, these projects pay for themselves (and more, according to George's observations). While some advocates of land taxation propose that the revenues be used toward funding a minimum income/national dividend, this would stop one of its key advantages from being realized. Instead, a ULT in its entirety would be used to fund national and regional governments. If government were dependent on the ULT for its funding, it would be incentivized to build the best possible infrastructure and government services, which would further increase its revenues. It would keep the budgets balanced, and improve location access for all.

In line with these same principles of land/locations having a public aspect to them, the New Physiocrats also advocate the Freedom to Roam laws, as implemented in Northern Europe. These laws allow for the public to have access to privately owned wilderness. It is to the benefit of hikers, campers, and boaters who set out to explore and enjoy the nature in their country. Right to Light laws may be of similar interest, which protect homes and public parks from having their natural light blocked by man-made structures.

From a practical standpoint, it may be necessary to temporarily compensate those most affected by the ULT, and give ample time to prepare citizens for its implementation. To address the political unpopularity of sending citizens a tax bill, it would be best to collect these taxes directly from paid salaries, similar to an income tax. Citizens would still see dramatic salary increases immediately (due to the shift away from income taxes, and the other New Physiocratic Programs), but the benefits would become even more pronounced once people adjust their behavior to reflect the new incentives.

Environmental Taxation

Nature grants us air and water just as it does land, yet the costs of using these resources are often not accounted for. The air is ours to breathe, and allowing the unfettered use of the air outside is no different than allowing someone to leave their car on inside your home, filling it with fumes. In line with the same principles that justify the taxation of land, the same treatment should apply to air and water. A tax must be levied on the use of air in the form of pollution taxes in order to account for the costs of hazardous emissions. In order to not saddle producers with costs which will render them uncompetitive, the revenues raised from these particular taxes should be fully returned to industry by directing the funds toward capacity for inexpensive, abundant, clean energy, and technologies. The revenues would go directly into the Electrical Energy Bank, paying for the fixed costs of power production, thereby maintaining energy affordability. Likewise, the use of coastal territory for fishing must be taxed in a similar manner, with the revenues raised directed toward funding for sustainable aquaculture development, funded through the Agricultural Bank. These costs must also be accounted for with imported products.

Using taxation in these areas to factor in the costs of using publicly inherited resources creates incentives for market-based solutions. The money raised can then effectively be used to provide funding for these solutions and grow the economy. The alternative of using a purely regulatory approach keeps a lid on economic growth, allows room for loopholes, and ties up courts. Rules, when they do need to be in place, need appropriate cost-benefit analysis, and may require creative solutions. If water used for fracking, for example, is required to be sourced from solar powered desalinization plants, or an environmentally friendly water capture method, it may aid both the environment and the economy by spurring new industry.

Returning the Money You Earned

As land, air, resources, and the environment are inherited from nature, their rents should be treated communally. Labor, by contrast, is earned — whether from your work as an employee, from your innovations, or from your business operations. Not only is it unfair for your efforts to be taxed, it's also economically unwise. Taxing your labor discourages you from working harder, and taxing corporate income discourages business activity and investment. Burdening people's efforts with taxes makes the economic system unsustainable by sapping its energy, while it's forced to support an aging population and absorb external shocks.

The New Physiocratic system returns these tax revenues to where they belong: you, the labor force, and the business organizations who produced this wealth in the first place.

While classical Georgist theory advocates eliminating corporate and personal income taxation altogether, the New Physiocrats advocate a different approach, taking into account the realities of modern societies and economies. The platform of the New Physiocrats returns the fruits of your labor through the National Income Supplement (NIS). After collecting income taxes, the NIS pays them back as a cash transfer to workers, where the average income earner receives the full amount.

Efforts at corporate taxation are often futile, as the capital and income which are taxed are very mobile, and can quickly flee burdensome taxes and regulatory environments. Often companies can import goods and services to where the demand is, allowing them to operate from anywhere in the world while avoiding or minimizing tariffs. Corporate income tax makes for a poor source of revenue, and is better used to incentivize particular behaviors and steer a country's limited resources toward desired activities and goals. Taxes on retail service-sector businesses are harder to evade, as shops cannot be moved abroad, unlike factories and offices. However, added costs for retail outlets can be passed on to consumers, and must be applied carefully to avoid cost increases on basic needs, such as food. Rates must be very low, and revenue raised from corporate taxation must be entirely returned to businesses; and done so in a way that steers nations' resources toward its goals of providing affordable essentials for the entire population.

Personal income tax must be simplified, flattened, remove deductions, and collected without the need to file tax declarations. The costs of its administration must be kept to a bare minimum, and should be implemented with the help of e-governance (as in the Estonian model). Tax brackets must be linked to national income percentiles rather than exact values, to avoid bracket creep.

Relying on income taxation to fund general government revenues is dangerous, especially in countries with aging populations. The shrinking labor force in the private sector has to sustain a growing segment of the population in retirement, the disabled, the unemployed, and the underemployed. It is an increasingly heavy burden on the continuously shrinking labor force, which sees no end in sight to the tax increases. Meanwhile, the retired and the disadvantaged are left at risk, not knowing when their economic support base might topple under its own weight.

All corporate taxes collected must be distributed directly back to businesses. Likewise, all personal income taxes collected must then be divided and distributed back to the labor force as part of an income supplement program (to be discussed in the following sections). The New Physiocrats refer to such a benefit as the National Income Supplement. This has several advantages over traditional welfare schemes to reduce poverty:

- It is the most direct and certain means of achieving income redistribution, which is often a goal of government regardless
- It achieves redistribution with the most minimal possible tax burden on all income earners
- All workers see an increase in their income when rising productivity rates and automation benefit select groups in the workforce; it promotes harmony across socioeconomic classes, as a portion of all incomes would be put into the NIS pool, then paid out
- Workers from every income bracket would cheer for income growth in other income brackets, as they would also benefit from their growth

- If the labor force uses the income supplement to move into lower-paying roles, the income supplement amount lowers automatically (as there will be a smaller total national contribution); thereby disincentivizing that sort of negative behavior
- As it is not a defined benefit payment program, it ensures that the program never runs a deficit
- The money goes directly to workers, rather than through opaque, wasteful, government programs
- Citizens experience the effects of economic outcomes immediately via direct deposits in their bank accounts

Instead of trying to affect living standards (and income distribution) through complicated, often wasteful schemes, along with minimum wage laws and unions, this method provides the most efficient and direct way of achieving the same desired effect. The National Income Supplement would replace the minimum wage. At the same time, it's a system that boosts incomes on all levels; lower tax rates on the top, and steeply negative tax rates on the bottom. This system provides powerful incentives to enter the labor force, and allows each income bracket to share the success of the others, promoting harmony between the classes. It allows all people to immediately benefit from the country's economic success immediately, visible in their bank accounts, rather than waiting indefinitely for policies to bear fruit to them directly.

The New Management Incentives

Corporate upper management must have its incentives aligned to the long-term health of the companies and stakeholders that they serve. Too often, directors are not beholden to the long-term interests of their shareholders, nor the economic success of the nation. Compensation is determined by the directors themselves and allows for a disconnect between compensation and performance. When salaries are more closely tied to performance, it tends to be short-term performance, while often sacrificing the long-term health of the firms. Salary caps are a dangerous solution like all price and wage controls, and would result in skilled management leaving for places without caps. Instead, by law, a sizeable portion of executive compensation, including non-cash benefits, should be in the form of long-term shareholdings, which can be sold after 5+ years. The interests of other shareholders would already be tied to the longer-term interests of the company through tax incentives we would apply to capital gains as part of the Assisted Savings Program. This would involve taxing capital gains in a way to incentivize shareholders to also hold shares for 5+ years, become invested in the long-term health of their companies, and favoring domestic investment.

Voting shareholders must have a binding say on executive compensation, to ensure no perverse incentives for the board of directors. However, with shareholder meetings so distant and inaccessible, there must also be an easier way for shareholders to communicate their feedback and ideas with company directors. A country's securities regulator must host an online forum for each listed company in which shareholders can voice their opinions, and form groups to elect and influence the boards. It would also provide opportunities for the boards to respond directly to any concerns.

There must be a surtax on companies with excessive executive pay ratios (in addition to on the executives themselves). This would mean that it would make more financial sense for companies to raise salaries of their workers. The funds raised from the surtax would go toward the National Income Supplement, so that regardless of whether the companies make the decision to raise salaries or not, the labor force benefits. With the suggested income tax rates of 8, 16, and 24 percent (before the Three Pillars are paid out), a tax rate on executives beyond a certain pay ratio within their company would add on a new tax bracket, at a rate of 32 percent for income earned beyond the breach of the ratio. When executive pay breaches the limit, the company itself would see a surtax of 2 percent in addition to the normal rate of 8 percent. This surtax would also be returned to the labor force via the NIS.

The disadvantage of using executive pay ratios as a metric, is that these incentives could encourage companies to shed their lower wage workers altogether. The incentive would therefore need to be conditional on a certain percentage of the company's workforce being comprised of lower income individuals. Calculating the pay ratio would also need to include work that is contracted out to other firms, to prevent companies from splitting up to meet the requirements.

Monopolies and Public-Private Partnerships

Monopolies must be avoided as much as possible, as they are a form of economic privilege, which are typically detrimental to the broader economy (namely in the form of lower efficiency and incomes, and higher prices). In many countries, even with so-called natural monopolies such as the electrical grid, policymakers have found ways to create competition, to the benefit of consumers. These competitive markets must be encouraged as much as possible. However, in instances where a natural monopoly cannot be avoided, the monopoly businesses must be majority-owned by the public, at arms-length from the government. This can be done through majority ownership by the country's sovereign wealth fund, with a constitutional cap on private ownership (likely to approximately a quarter of the shares). Profits would be regulated, as is standard with monopoly enterprises worldwide, and would be taxed at the top rate (of 24%); distributed evenly to the Three Pillars and Sectoral Banks, under the same regime as financial sector profits. The remainder would be reinvested or returned to the shareholders. By operating at arms-length from government, with some limited private ownership, and perhaps private management, it would help discourage resource waste. Yet the effects of monopoly would be mitigated through this form of compensation.

Public-private partnerships can theoretically be beneficial to taxpayers by introducing the most recent methods and technologies, and operating more efficiently, at lower cost. In contrast, government workers are theoretically more expensive and unionized, less responsive to change, and less efficient. However, in practice, public-private partnerships are often not as transparent as they should be, with tenders offered by friends and supporters of the politicians, and large cost overruns. Private bidding for public projects is sometimes necessary and should be an option. However, the government should retain the means to take on contracts themselves, and the public (along with the publicly elected anti-corruption agency) should hold have the right to veto public-private partnerships that are on the table. Furthermore, with union activity removed from public enterprise, public works companies would be more flexible, inexpensive, and able to compete on the market with private contractors.

Sustainable Value Added Tax (SVAT)

Although people who are outside the labor force (e.g., retirees, those unable/unwilling to work, etc.) cannot contribute to their societal costs via income taxation, they do contribute to economic activity and tax revenues through consumption, as do the unemployed. In short, those who are not working are still spending. However, without collecting some of their contribution in the form of taxation, the shrinking labor force is left to shoulder the financial responsibility. As the proportion of retirees rises, and more people exit the labor force for various other reasons, this burden becomes increasingly large. It is unfair that previous generations that got away with lighter taxation, and the successive generations' labor force is left with the financial burden from worsening demographics and structural underemployment. Consumption taxes (such as a VAT) ensure that the entire population, regardless of age or employment status, is contributing their share. A sustainable VAT (SVAT) would do so while accounting for the externalities of transactions.

It can be said that people consume a vast amount of goods and services — sometimes excessively. It cannot be objectively judged what exactly constitutes excessive consumption. However, rising obesity rates, unserviceable amounts of consumer debt, large trade and current account deficits, overburdened landfills, and depletion of scarce resources are all indicators of how much a country can consume compared to its capacity to produce, and its capacity to deal with its environmental consequences. They are in fact all serious issues, not only indicators. These issues also carry a real financial cost to a country and its economic, health care and financial systems. Consumption, though an essential component of the economic system, can have a societal cost in some instances. A VAT whose burden falls on the end consumers, can account for the costs of its externalities. Henry George, while in principle was against taxation aside from taxes on land/ locations (and perhaps on other monopolies), recognized that the natural world we inherit has intrinsic and not only instrumental value. A broad value added tax prices in the true costs of consumption and its externalities to nature and society. A rate reduction could be applied for recycled or repaired goods, and a zero rate would apply to basic goods and their inputs, encouraging positive rather than negative externalities.

In the current global trade regime, countries without a VAT have their exports unfairly penalized, while effectively subsidizing imports. By taxing consumption to relieve the tax burden on producers, domestic consumption is suppressed to the benefit of exporters. All goods and services sold domestically are taxed in a VAT regime, while exports are zero-rated. However, because goods and services that are both produced and sold domestically are taxed equally under a VAT, it is also far less distortionary than trade tariffs. These consumption taxes also capture revenues from tourists and visitors, who use infrastructure with otherwise inadequate compensation to their host country.

Types of Consumption

Consumption can be classified in various ways; however, for the purpose of this discussion, let's classify goods/services in the following categories:

- Basic Essentials
- Luxuries accessible to few
- Cultural goods
- Goods with particularly large negative externalities
- Everything else

We define Basic Essentials as goods necessary for basic human survival, which are required in specific, measured amounts. These include food, water, and shelter. Luxury goods would include those that are *only* consumed by the top tier of income earners, such as high-end jewellery. Importing these luxuries drains foreign currency reserves at the expense of importing capital equipment. Goods with particularly large externalities include tobacco, recreational drugs, simple sugars, fuels, and aerosols. Cultural goods include local handicrafts, cottage industry, art, and performances of local/national cultural significance. All other goods and services would occupy the middle ground. With this in mind, a progressive and sustainable VAT, an SVAT, can emerge to fund the remainder of government that the Unified Location Tax does not.

The costs of Basic Essentials must be kept to a minimum to maximize real incomes; not only with regards to the SVAT program, but by keeping supply high, supply chains fluid and without interruption, infrastructure adequate, competition intense, and ample transport options for products to get to market. With regards to the SVAT, this means a zero-rate on essential goods. For the New Physiocrats, this is limited to fresh ingredients and specific prepared food, housing, water, and culturally significant clothing. Specific details will be discussed in the following section.

Focus on Purchasing Power

When the topics of wages and government benefits are discussed, the question always arises as to what is an adequate income for a person to survive, or perhaps thrive. There are also questions about how these programs in themselves might actually drive up the cost of living. These questions are highly relevant to the platform of the New Physiocrats, as it pertains to the Three Pillars program among other policies.

The nominal value of a person's income is meaningless without the context of purchasing power. In some countries, a very small nominal income can afford one a luxurious life, while in other countries a very large nominal income may be inadequate to pay rent. Rising incomes do not help people if prices are rising faster than these incomes. It will not matter what income the New Physiocratic platform and the Three Pillars provide unless we can ensure that this income has an adequate (and growing) purchasing power. Therefore, these programs only provide meaningful results if they are matched with a concerted effort to drive down the cost of essential goods and services (without promoting waste and misuse). With housing becoming increasingly unaffordable, we see the need for these efforts becoming more critical. Governments have long focused on other economic metrics, but have largely ignored purchasing power; particularly the purchasing power for the most necessary essential goods. Rising GDP growth means little to someone facing soaring housing and food costs.

The merits of reducing the cost of all goods in aggregate are debatable, and reducing prices on different goods and services would benefit different segments of the population. However, reducing the cost of the basic essentials for survival is a certain way to increase the purchasing power of the entire population. At a minimum, these basic essentials include housing, food, water, clothing, electricity, transportation, retail banking, and perhaps communications.

To decrease prices for these essentials, there must be a dramatic increase in domestic supply, competition, and rational use. The most modern and efficient methods must also be employed to reduce costs. This might require an increase in aid and lending to these sectors, and for the tax system to encourage new entrants into the market. Representatives in these sectors also must have a permanent channel in which to discuss with the government and the public, necessary infrastructure, and strategies to reduce prices. The billions currently spent on subsidized housing, subsidized mortgages, and affordable housing development are wasted, as they don't address the root of the issue; lack of supply, property kept out of the market, perverse tax incentives, excessive lending for property purchases, etc.

How do you justify (economically) reallocating resources from sectors that the market determines to produce the most wealth, to these other sectors? Economic development often drives up prices for these Basic Essentials, negating the positive effects of growth. Having a system to automatically redistribute resources from high growth areas to the production of basic essentials would maintain purchasing power for everyone. Furthermore, as there is always demand for basic goods, supporting the Static Sectors for Basic Goods provides the economy industries to fall back on when Dynamic Sectors change or flounder.

These reallocations must be made by returning corporate tax revenues back to businesses via Sectoral Banks. This is one of the chief automatic mechanisms through which the Physiocratic goals can be met, without the politicization of picking winners.

Sectoral Banks

By the mid-late 2010s, we saw corporate profits worldwide were soaring to new records, to the benefit of very few. Most of this money was held in cash, not reinvested, nor used for hiring or wage increases. Under a New Physiocratic regime, we would see this translated into greater purchasing power for the entire population, while at the same time returning the tax revenues that businesses worked to earn through their efforts. The two seemingly conflicting sides of the equation would be reconciled through what we call, Sectoral Banks. It would also overlap with the Georgist principles of relieving taxes from earned income. With the New Physiocrats' Assisted Savings Program already channeling capital gains and dividend tax revenues to the population as direct cash transfers, these Sectoral Banks would guarantee that these cash transfers have real purchasing power.

Sectoral Banks and some of the industries that own them, would need to be kick-started by government in their initial phase. This would also include the technical capacity for their educational facilities, and in some cases industrial capacity as well.

Typically in developed economies we see disproportionate profit growth in a small handful of economic sectors. Recently these have been finance, resource extraction, tourism, and technology services. This has created a situation in which many economies lack diversification, rely on a handful of unstable sectors, hollow out their static sectors, and hurt cultures and traditional ways of life. By ensuring balanced development with diversification between [and within] sectors, and the promotion of new businesses, the economy will be far better placed to find new paths for growth in the event of shock or rapid change. At the same time, the production of basic essentials for living (for which there is always a demand), will be maintained as economic sectors, and serve as industries on which an economy can fall back on in times of need.

The word 'country' is used loosely in this section, and would also be applicable to labor market and customs unions, and other common markets, which jointly collect tariff revenues.

Sectoral Banks must be part of the toolset and automatic mechanisms in a New Physiocratic government which are employed for the following purposes:

- A means to return corporate tax revenues back to businesses
- To provide support to strategic sectors of business and society
- Put downward pressure on prices of Basic Essentials, by increasing their supply through substantial capitalization for their investment
- Creating mechanisms with which funds are automatically channeled to the appropriate segments of the economy to deal with economic changes as they arise
- Providing training for people who are employed or wish to be employed in each respective sector
- A means with which companies within in each sector can share capital equipment

- Allows companies to join forces to buy capital equipment at bulk purchase prices
- Establishing a means to pool resources so that each sector can develop a strategy for long-term success
- A channel for funds to circulate to all economic sectors when one specific sector is booming (typically oil and mineral resources); thereby addressing Dutch Disease

Sectoral Banks must be owned by the sectors they represent. For cxample, all farms would be owners of the Agricultural Bank. To achieve their goals effectively, certain rules must be instituted:

- Businesses holding shares in Sectoral Banks must meet domestic residency requirements for directors' residency, domestic operations, profits, stock listings, and corporate headquarters; foreign companies would need to set up local companies to apply
- The banks could only offer their loans, ownership, dividends, and training strictly to their own sectors
- Although shareholders in the banks could not receive the benefits from Sectoral Banks outside their sectors, they would be free to take loans from independent banks
- Some economic groups would be shareholders in multiple banks (e.g., farms would hold shares in both the Agricultural Bank as well as the Bank of Basic Essentials)
- Dividends are to be paid from Sectoral Banks' profits, not from the funds they receive from tax revenues
- New entrants must be allowed as shareholders immediately, but only entitled to dividends after beginning operations
- Shareholdings should increase with output, then capped at a certain point; with the mandate of safeguarding competition and new entrants
- Each bank must own and operate educational facilities with which to train their labor force for their own sector
- Individual bank branches would have a degree of autonomy, and invest a portion of their funds locally
- Communities could petition for a Sectoral Bank branch in their area
- The banks cannot be a means to form cartels of any kind, and could not force industry groups to become members, nor their

members to join in group purchase or sale initiatives; enforced by an elected, independent investigative agency

- The banks could not restrict the entrance of new companies to becoming owning members
- The unused portion of distributed funds that each Sectoral Bank receives would be taxed at a rate of 2% per year (with a 2-year exemption), and redistributed evenly among all the Sectoral Banks
- Transparency must be guaranteed in management meetings and reporting for Sectoral Banks, safeguarding public visibility of their operations
- Each bank must include its own venture capital fund, for which they are entitled to use half of its funding, in order to ensure no artificial preference between debt and equity financing

All corporate income taxes that would be raised, aside from the special cases discussed, must be redistributed evenly across all Sectoral Banks. In addition to this source of funding, each bank would have their own separate streams of funding from various taxation sources.

The following banks would be established:

- Resource Exploration Bank
- Agricultural Bank
- Manufacturing Bank
- Basic Essentials Bank
- Startup Bank
- National Defense Bank
- Strategic Technology Bank
- Infrastructure Bank
- Infrastructure Industry Bank
- Electrical Energy Bank
- Export Development Bank
- Cultural Bank
- Network of Regional Credit Unions
- Housing Bank
- Consumers Bank
- Regional Development Bank

Resource Exploration Bank:

As the name suggests, this bank would be mandated with funding resource exploration projects, and initiate the first steps of the extraction process. Owned by the nation's resource extraction and exploration companies, it would house the related educational and resource houses for these endeavours, and train the required labor force. It would ensure that when resource prices are low, exploration and the groundwork continues in preparation for upward price and demand shocks. When resource prices rise, tax rates on this sector would automatically rise too, and this bank would also ensure ample investment in response to these changes.

Agricultural Bank:

The Agricultural Bank would be owned by all registered farms, as defined by a certain value of agricultural inputs and outputs. As one of the keystone Sectoral Banks, it would have ownership of factories for value-added agricultural manufacturing (such as processing and packaging facilities), enough to meet the entire agricultural export capacity. In addition, its regional branches would own the farmers' section of the Local Markets as well as the licensed Farmers' Shops. It would receive funding from not only the pool of corporate tax revenues, but also revenue from agricultural import and export tariffs. When global food prices rise, so would these revenues, and farmers would be awash in resources to respond, insulating domestic consumers from the shock.

Manufacturing Bank:

The Manufacturing Bank, owned by the nation's manufacturers, would play an important role in mitigating the effects of Dutch Disease. For example, if there is a spike in the price of oil in a major exporter, typically a country's manufacturing sector is hollowed out as a strengthening currency renders it uncompetitive, and the country's resources race toward the oil sector. With some of the tax revenues from such a boom (as in any other sector) being automatically diverted toward the Manufacturing Bank, the sector would be given a lifeline as the rising tide of other sectors would also pay dividends to manufacturers. The bank would also receive the compensatory tariff revenues from non-Basic Essential manufactured goods. The bank would also be in charge of a manufacturing training program.

Basic Essentials Bank:

The Basic Essentials bank, owned by the nation's farmers and manufacturers of the other essentials for living and their subcomponents (e.g., agricultural equipment), may also be partly owned by some businesses, which also own shares in the Manufacturing Bank and Agricultural Bank. The bank's mandate, coordinated with the Effort to Support Purchasing power, would be to provide the lowest possible consumer prices for these Basic Essentials (without sacrificing quality), and a degree of self-reliance in Static Sectors. It would also receive the import and export tariff revenues for these products that are applied under the compensatory trade regime. Like the Manufacturing Bank, the Basic Essentials Bank would have its own education and training program.

Startup Bank:

The Startup Bank would be owned by all domestic businesses that are under 5 years old (regardless of their financial success) and are not associated with any existing business; one owner could not increase shareholdings by registering multiple businesses. Businesses would receive a share upon registering, and their holding would increase after the first year, and decrease again by the final year. This would ensure the legitimacy of the businesses in the pool, and then wean their dependence from funding. The bank would also handle a program for venture capital, based on Israel's Yomza program and their Innovation Authority. The goal of the Startup Bank would be to achieve measurable goals related to the number, success, and funding of new businesses, and to allow them to achieve profitability by the end of their 5-year ownership period. This would dramatically ramp up competition across the economy and allow entrepreneurs to move up the social ladder.

National Defense Bank:

The National Defense Bank would use its funds for companies whose efforts are focused on researching or producing hardware specifically to meet the needs of the unique security requirements of the country. This bank would also operate an engineering university, so that young, creative minds can gain relevant experience for their careers while at the same time providing a source of inexpensive R&D for the military and police to reduce the burden on taxpayers. It would be unable to finance military operations of any kind, and would have a mandate of spurring dual-use (military and civilian) innovations, and achieving national self-reliance in military hardware. The New Physiocrats view national security as an essential precursor to investment, peace, and life.

Strategic Technology Bank:

The Strategic Technology Bank would be mandated to fund businesses focused on developing new technology, as defined by their domestic research and development spending, number of patents, and patent expansion rate, versus the company size. The purpose of this bank would be to provide a counterweight to the Static Sectors of Basic Essentials, by providing the economy with an equal amount of dynamism and healthy risk. By maintaining ample funding for companies which prove themselves to be innovative, the economy will be ready to seize new opportunities as economic conditions change. This bank would also own a cutting edge post-secondary institution to bring together students who are motivated to enter innovative professions and patent new ideas.

Infrastructure Bank:

The Infrastructure Bank would be a bank owned by the government's sovereign wealth fund. Its sole mandate would be so that national and regional governments could borrow from the bank to fund infrastructure projects, and its ownership structure would ensure that the bank operates at arms-length from the government on a for-profit basis. With the ULT in place, the rise in land values after infrastructure investments would then be collected, making repayment straightforward. As the interest on the repaid funds would return to the governments via the sovereign wealth fund, infrastructure investment would flourish.

Infrastructure Industry Bank

The Infrastructure Industry Bank would be owned by companies involved in producing raw materials, equipment, and final goods for creating infrastructure. It would be a diverse group of companies, from railcar and railroad manufacturers, to concrete and excavator producers. Its mandate would be to ensure that the supply side of infrastructure can be met, and with a degree of self-reliance for such essentials, to control potential supply constraints and infrastructure cost overruns.

Electrical Energy Bank:

The Electrical Energy Bank would be a bank owned by the nation's renewable energy suppliers. In addition to the standard pool of funds from corporate tax revenues, this bank would also be capitalized by the greenhouse gas and pollution taxes that would be levied on unclean sources of energy. This would help ensure the development of clean energy infrastructure and enable the conditions for low consumer and industrial energy prices.

Export Development Bank:

The Export Development Bank would be owned by companies whose revenues are mainly derived from exports, or those requesting funding specifically to meet goals in export growth. Mandated with promoting exports, the bank would offer export financing and trade credit insurance, as other export banks around the world. By designating this bank as a Sectoral Bank, connected to the pool of corporate taxation funds, it would ensure that as a country's incomes grow, its current account balance remains stable.

The Cultural Bank

The Cultural Bank would be owned by the country's artists, musicians, craftsmen, media outlets, community restaurants, and artisans (like those found in the Local Markets). This bank would also own a diverse range of media outlets specifically for music, movies, art displays, and entertainment media, in addition to its ownership of the artisan section of the Local Markets. As with most of the Sectoral Banks, the new entrants would be granted a slightly disproportionate share in the bank, so that incumbents don't always hold their market share captive. In addition, a tax on media spectrum (such as radio spectrum and communications infrastructure oligopolies), would be distributed directly to the Cultural Bank. The Cultural Bank would also be obligated to offer educational facilities for traditional crafts, cooking, and other cultural arts. This bank ensures that as the economy advances and businesses grow, culture and traditional lifestyle are not left behind.

Network of Regional Credit Unions

The National Union of Credit Unions would be owned by the regional credit unions, which in turn would be owned by their bank account holders. Each governing region would have its own autonomous credit union, and would be capitalized with the aid of its share of the corporate taxation funds distributed to all Sectoral Banks. These funds could also be used to pay for their fixed costs for meeting their mandate. The credit unions under this program would be limited to offering basic banking and brokerage services, such as bank accounts, ASP accounts, and business loans. The banks would have limitations with regards to offering mortgages, in that property loans could only be offered for business purposes.

Under the New Physiocratic constitution, citizens would be entitled to bank accounts and investment accounts, which would be necessary to administer the programs under the Three Pillars. By granting ownership of these institutions to its users, costs to consumers would be minimized. The mandate of the Network of Regional Credit unions would be to ensure all citizens have access to a bank account and ASP account. A positive externality of distributing the funds evenly across each regional credit union would be that a slightly outsized volume of capital would enter less populated regions, thereby automatically creating more even development, and by its very nature would magnify the achievements of the Regional Development Bank.

Housing Bank

The Housing Bank would be owned by entities that are licensed specifically to build affordable housing, as defined by rental price per square meter as a percentage of median income. The funds could insure a portion of the of the loan values (for the builders, not the purchasers), in addition to normal lending operations. Its mandate would be to maximize the number of homes built within the affordable classification, while maintaining architectural and environmental standards. As corporate tax revenues grow, the funding for the Housing Banks (as with the other Sectoral Banks) would therefore grow too. This would ensure a healthy supply of housing to supply the citizens in a growing economy, while maintaining their purchasing power.

Consumers Bank:

The Consumers Bank would be structured like a consumers' co-op, (such as the UK's Co-operative Group) held by all citizen-residents, and would own farms, agricultural processing and packaging facilities (enough to meet the most basic level of domestic demand), the Consumers section of Local Markets, and a chain of Basic Essentials shops. It would also hold the Renters Union, giving tenants greater power to negotiate their rent. In addition, it would house some consumer regulatory bodies (which would be funded outside of the Sectoral Banking system) to ensure consumer safety, labelling transparency, and product longevity. Giving a consumer-owned organization a strong presence in the retail market for Basic Essentials (with an element of vertical integration) tips the balance of economic power in favor of those in need of greater purchasing power for these goods.

Regional Development Bank

The Regional Development Bank would be owned jointly by the country's regional governing bodies, allowing regions to engage in development projects which could then be repaid from rising ULT revenues. Without a regional development effort, small cities, towns, and villages end up losing their populations, while people become concentrated in a limited number of urban areas. While concentrated cities have their benefits (as discussed), an imbalance between urban and rural regions creates its own social and economic issues. A loss of rural life can lead to brain drain from the critical agricultural sector, as well as losses of traditional culture and lifestyles. Encouraging regional development also helps take luck out of the equation when it comes to the benefits of being born in a certain location. Bank branches would be divided by region, and would have autonomy for the loans they issue. The public would have the power within their own regions to impeach, charge, and replace their local branch management via petition. This would be a preventative measure against corruption and patronage.

This bank would not only be mandated to ensure even development across regions, but also to operate at a profit.

Agricultural Bank and Consumers Bank – Privileges and Responsibilities

Both the Agricultural Bank and Consumers Bank would be founded with ownership in agricultural equipment and processing companies (the Consumers Bank would also own some farms itself). These Sectoral Banks would be granted the privilege to increase their shareholdings in agricultural equipment and processing companies, and invest in these firms while being exempt from taxes on capital gains and dividends earned from these companies. This would ensure that gains from adding value in agriculture would accrue both to farmers and consumers, and both groups could make the appropriate decisions in their own interest, for which they have their responsibilities. The Consumers Bank would also be granted these same privileges for ownership in affordable homebuilding companies, to the same effect.

Business-to-Business Portal

The Sectoral Banks would jointly own a business-to-business portal, in the style of Alibaba: a one-stop-shop where companies can find a factory or farm to procure the products they need. The importance of such a service should not be understated. In China, it has contributed tremendously to the success of manufacturers, and has made the operations of business that rely on them, far easier. Opening such a channel for businesses to trade, would be a boon for the economy.

With the Sectoral Banks in place, corporate taxes would be returned to business, in line with Georgist principles and those of the New Physiocrats. Growing corporate profits would translate into balanced, broad-based growth in all sectors and regions. With all cylinders firing in unison, the positive effects of growth would be felt by all, with the most minimal possible tax burden, with minimal state ownership, and with substantial growth in consumer purchasing power. The resulting economic diversification would mean an economy that is prepared for any shock or opportunity that may arise. As the mechanism for distributing the funds in the Sectoral Bank system would be automatic, the opportunities for lobbying, subsidy requests, and corruption would be replaced with a fair means of support for business.

The unused portion of the funds that would be distributed to the Sectoral Banks, would be taxed (as described above) and redistributed evenly amongst the Sectoral Banks again. This ensures that capital would always be automatically distributed to the sectors where there is a demand for investment, instead of collecting in pools of unutilized cash.

In the case of customs unions and various other forms of political-economic unions (such as the EU), these principles could still be applied, with each country having its own set of Sectoral Banks. However, the New Physiocratic rules would mean that revenues from sources such as trade tariffs and taxes on short-term capital inflows would have to be distributed to each country by the overarching governing body. If distributed according to population (as opposed to economic output), this may achieve a small but important redistributional effect, and would aid in the industrialization and modernization process.

The Effort to Support Purchasing Power — Benefit Licenses

The second method to increase purchasing power, proposed by the New Physiocrats, is to encourage the sale of low-price Basic Essentials at the point of consumption. It is not enough to foster increased production of Basic Essentials; it must be ensured that the retail/distribution networks are in place to distribute them, and to ensure that low costs are carried through to consumers. Without outlets and distribution networks to circulate the increased supply, the availability becomes limited, the lower prices become hidden, and if there is a VAT placed on these goods, the benefits become further negated.

We refer to the agency with the mandate of using this method, as the Effort to Support Purchasing Power. The same agency would also have the authority to take anti-trust measures to meet these same goals.

Special licenses must be granted to retail businesses that meet certain requirements, for their role in distributing Basic Essentials. We can preface this section by saying there must be no restrictions on these businesses on operating before their licenses are granted; the licenses would only grant these businesses special privileges. These licenses would allow them to take ownership in an additional Sectoral Bank, the Bank of Basic Essentials. As this bank would be one of those receiving funds from the Sectoral Bank program, from the pool of corporate income tax revenues, it would be able to offer a combination of inexpensive loans, training and schooling, and cash dividends.

To achieve the desired effect, Basic Essentials (e.g., fresh foods), regardless of which outlet they're sold from, would be relieved of VAT. Restaurants play a special role in the distribution of food as well, as they and the cuisine they prepare are also a manifestation of the region's culture. Certain clothing can play a similar role. As mentioned earlier, while the LVT component of the ULT brings physical structures and establishments up from the earth, and the building tax component of the ULT moulds the structures, like an artist molding clay. If these structures were defined by the type and price of products they sell, it becomes possible to encourage the development not only of affordable housing, but also of affordable clothing and food relevant to the regional culture. The use of licenses here would also swiftly eliminate VAT compliance costs.

Community Restaurants, Cultural Clothing, and Groceries

For example, we can define a cooked meal that uses 95% of its ingredients [by weight] sourced within the same state/province as pertaining to regional culture. We can also call this meal affordable if it's priced at 0.0125% of the national median annual income, and contains a particular nutritional value. If a restaurant exclusively serving meals that meet these requirements was then given a license, which allowed it to offer its products without VAT, and an exemption on a building tax portion of the ULT, there would be a powerful incentive for a network of affordable, cultural food proprietors to form. The same can be applied to clothing, another Basic Essential with a cultural component. Combined with efficient use of land and superior infrastructure (as a result of the ULT), subsidized labor (from the NIS), and financial backing for both their own businesses and those providing their raw materials (through Sectoral Banks), the License Benefit would drive down prices for Basic Essentials, maximizing consumer purchasing power. As stated in the ULT section, a building tax component of the ULT would vary from 0 to 0.5% depending on the percentage of the space comprised of Basic Essentials (including affordable housing).

The New Physiocrats' platform does endorse these Benefit Licenses for restaurants and clothing shops, which meet requirements for affordability, regional cultural significance, and locally sourced production. This would be the same with grocery stores which meet and sell strictly Basic Essentials, and meet these same requirements. The key to the success in this program — as always — would be the precondition of transparency. There must be a public registry of the details of how each business is meeting these requirements, and the license must be on display to the public. The Effort to Support Purchasing Power must be able to have a forced election for its leadership if the public petitions it to do so.

Local Markets

There is a certain allure to farmers' markets, souks, bazaars, and similar public marketplaces where one can get lost, use all of one's senses, and experience the local culture. These markets exist in almost every culture, and are often the main places where chefs go for inspiration, tourists go for the complete cultural experience, and locals go to find their preferred foods and small consumer goods. Sadly, the age of the automobile in some places has resulted in large supermarkets becoming the more practical choice, at the expense of culture, character, and inspiration. While the ULT and other New Physiocratic policies might reverse some of this change (partly by increasing density in urban areas), there is also an opportunity to use these Local Markets as a means to keep prices low and boost purchasing power for Basic Essentials.

The New Physiocrats envision a law ensuring that every community or district that meets certain population or density criteria has space allocated for their own Local Market. These structures would be built to the highest standards of beauty and quality in the official regional architectural style. Each market must be large, multi-floored, and divided into three parts: The Farmers' Market, the Patrons' Market, and the Artisans' Market. These would be owned by regional branches of the Agricultural Bank, the Consumers Bank, and the Cultural Bank respectively. There would be pre-cut allotted sizes for each shop, and no owner could operate more than one shop. The Farmers' Market and Patrons' Market would be limited to selling local food, while the Artisans' Market would be limited to selling goods that are manufactured on site (cottage industry).

The nexus of consumer-owned retail space, with incentives to minimize prices, and farmer-owned retail space—vertical integration

Image by ggrupa.pl

with no middleman—combined with an abundance of retail space and competition, would drive quality high and prices low. The Effort to Support Purchasing Power would determine the number, location, and size of these markets, forward looking to ensure ample retail space (therefore competition) for the foreseeable future. The mandate of this agency, as the name suggests, would be to keep prices low.

The Cultural Bank, owned by Artisans involved in cottage industry, would use these spaces to guarantee their craft. This would be a core element to the Effort to Maintain Tradition.

With the rent collected from these spaces collected by (and funding) their respective banks, the rent is essentially returning to the owners and supporting their sectors. As the structures themselves would be created by the Effort to Support Purchasing Power and the Effort to Maintain Tradition, the upfront costs to the retail businesses would be zero. The [upward] effect that these markets would have on land prices in the area would then increase ULT revenues, meaning these projects would pay for themselves.

Consumers and Farmers Shops

The Consumers Bank and Agricultural Bank would also own their own chains of food shops as well as farmland, with the same purpose as the markets:

- To increase purchasing power and quality for consumers
- To maximize farmers' profits by providing them with an opportunity to add value to their product, and to sell them at stable retail prices as opposed to unpredictable commodity prices.

The New Rules for Industrial Organization: The Problems with Picking Winners

"Picking Winners," as it's called in economic circles, is the process of governments deciding on certain sectors and promoting their growth. Typically, this is done with sectors that the government deems strategic, and takes the form of subsidies, trade protection, guaranteed loans, and other forms of directed credit.

For subsidies and credit to be directed toward specific industries, these resources must be taken from other industries, and the rest of society. Occasionally, governments do bet on a sector that manages to stand on its own two feet, and even thrive, but more typically this strategy results in a serious misallocation of resources. In China, it's easy to see immense overcapacity in many sectors, which become increasingly reliant on government directed credit to stay afloat. Meanwhile, other areas of the economy and small businesses are often starved of credit they need to grow.

Shipbuilding, automobiles, and electronics are common examples of industries that governments often deem strategic for various reasons; particularly in Asia's export-oriented economic regimes. Overcapacity, cheap credit, and subsidies may make these products artificially cheap, but they benefit those who are involved in those sectors, at the expense of everyone else. This preferred treatment creates an artificially high supply of products that do not necessarily benefit the broader population, using the resources that could have otherwise been used to make products that do; or at least ones that consumers demand. In some cases, such as agriculture, the subsidies are often combined with price floors, which create a situation where consumers are hit doubly hard, by both high prices as well as taxes to fund the subsidies.

Static, Dynamic, and Traditional Sectors

The demands of consumers often change, and products that seem to have insatiable demand one day, could prove fleeting the next. Tastes change, trends change, and fads come and go. The market adapts accordingly by producing goods and services to meet these changing demands, and with it the labor market adapts too.

However, there are some things for which consumer demand is much more stable — sometimes nearly static —because they are essential for human survival. The demand for food, water, clothing, and housing is universal among people, and although the quantities demanded may fluctuate, there is always a baseline demand for these goods. In a modern society, this may be (perhaps with some debate) expanded to include electricity, medicines, telecommunications, and transportation. Let's define the sectors producing these essentials as the Static Sectors.

The importance of Static Sectors is their effect on purchasing power. What good is a salary of 4000 per month without knowing whether your total cost of housing, food, and utilities is 3000 or 300? As the Static Sectors produce goods that every person needs, changes in the prices of these goods affect the broadest possible segment of the population and their purchasing power. Discussions about boosting wages are meaningless without putting the issues in the context of purchasing power.

We define Dynamic Sectors as those that produce products for whose demand (in aggregate) can change dramatically, or disappear quickly. This category particularly applies to many high-tech consumer items which can be easily displaced, as well as non-essentials and luxuries. The importance of these goods to a population's standard of living can be debated endlessly, but they differ from basic essentials in that they're not needed for survival, they don't have a guaranteed base level of demand, and they're more elastic. The Dynamic Sectors also tend to be the most productive, competitive, and efficient, and are imperative to a country's wealth.

Because everyone uses Static Sector goods, ensuring that the prices of these are as low as possible, would provide a boost in real incomes to the broadest possible segment of the population. Their prices are also felt the most by those in the lower ends of the income spectrum, in addition to the middle class. At the same time, as demand for these goods is especially stable, this area of the economy can act as a stabilizer and a floor to economic activity. While they may not necessarily be the most productive or profitable sectors for all countries, they are strategic for these reasons. There should be special effort to keep these goods as inexpensive as possible to maximize national purchasing power, and to maintain these areas of the economy for their stabilizing effects. Supporting Static Sectors is notably different from picking winners, as it is grounded in guaranteed demand and physical security concerns. Slight overcapacity in these sectors may even be beneficial to protect the public against price shocks.

An economy that's both stable and prosperous must have both Static and Dynamic Sectors, and the ability to shift resources from one sector to another, depending on the conditions in either. In times of hardship, having a Static Sector to fall back on is invaluable. In times where a country is well positioned to take advantage of innovation and change, the Dynamic Sectors take the leading role. A similar situation arises in the discussion of domestic versus export-oriented sectors. Preserving a country's Static Sectors prepares the economy for future shock, and employs those who are left behind when the Dynamic Sectors move full steam ahead.

Finally, we define Traditional Sectors as those producing goods or services with particular cultural significance to a country or region, and those that have a particular heritage. This appears quite subjective at first, but we will define it more explicitly in the next chapters. In a country like France, you could say cheese-making would fall under this category. Production of particular textiles, clothing, and handicrafts would also be appropriate for this classification for some countries. While preserving Traditional Sectors might be economically inefficient, as many of them are small-scale or cottage industries, they are significant contributors to a country's standard of living. One of the main reasons tourism thrives, and people spend vast amounts of money on travel, is to experience traditional local cultures. Although the value of experiencing architecture, cultural events, and traditional lifestyles is intangible, the prices that people are willing to pay for exposure to them is telling. Despite the immense wealth that the modern, globalized economy has provided, the intense backlash against open borders (for both trade and culture) only furthers the point about what people value. While on one hand people have embraced modernity, on the other hand people have felt an urge to seek something more. Yet the more the economy grows, the more we see cultures erode, and the population uses its new wealth to travel further and further afield to seek out culture. The New Physiocrats answer to this with the creation of a Cultural Bank, spaces for cottage industry, economic empowerment of rural areas, and legal mechanisms for tribal ownership of property.

Typically, any industry that is protected in some way, results in it being utterly inefficient, and produces an overpriced, lower quality product as a result of not being adequately exposed to competition. So how can we ensure the lowest possible prices for essentials, while maintaining the economy's Static Sectors?

Revenues from applied tariffs and taxes, must be returned to the Static Sectors which produce the country's essential goods. In addition, tax revenues from all other non-priority sectors, must be fed into the Static Sectors as well, and vice versa, so that both sectors are maintained. It must be done in a way that dramatically reduces costs, boosts supply and availability, while at the same time maintains intense competition, and does not harm the economy's Dynamic Sectors. It also must be applied transparently, and not to favored companies, as a traditional subsidy might do.

For a start, this means keeping corporate tax rates very low, so as not to damage the Dynamic Sectors, and to minimize the distortions that a corporate tax has on the economy. Tariffs necessary to maintain the country's Static Sectors must be kept at rates precisely high enough to compensate for unfair advantages of foreign competitors, and natural, or domestic regulatory disadvantages the domestic firms face. The rates must be low enough so that firms must still feel intense competitive pressures from abroad, and for the benefits of competition to be seen.

The Housing Union

Locations, unlike goods or services, are monopolies. Therefore, even with an abundance of housing (as a result of the New Physiocrats' policies), there is still an opportunity for monopolists to take advantage of consumers in a manner that's against the principles of a free market.

Image by ggrupa.pl

To mitigate this, we propose the Housing Union. This would be a portal in which renters or buyers who are obtaining housing from the same building, property owner, or developer, can join forces to receive a better deal, and to prevent landlord abuse.

Visual Space

While other forms of public space, such as air, earth, and waterways, are frequently topics of discussion, let's reflect on how much we value our visual space, and how much it contributes to the financial value of an area. A large portion of disposable income is spent on vacations; much of which is due to particular visual space. Whether it be a particular architecture, bright lights, sea views, mountain views, or other natural scenery, this visual space has a particular value. People pay a premium to live in a home with a pleasing view, and will fight developments that obstruct it. Although preferred visual space is somewhat subjective, consensus is seen in property values and tourism numbers. Properties with views of a park, waterfront, or mountain, are typically priced at a premium compared with equivalent properties with views of a billboard or side of a building. If a neighborhood has a few derelict buildings, the value of the rest of the properties also decreases significantly. By contrast, a neighborhood with comparable infrastructure and amenities, but where buildings are immaculate and styled in a widely enjoyed style of architecture, the entire neighborhood is valued higher. Similar principles can be applied to other aspects of visual space, including public infrastructure, cars, people, and fashion. This is in line with Georgist thinking of space being treated as a public good. Taking examples from other jurisdictions, outdoor billboards would be forbidden under the New Physiocratic platform, as a measure to reclaim our physical space. Regional architectural guidelines, which partly determine ULT rates, are guided by the same principles.

Clothing and housing are unique in that they are basic essentials for living, but also affect the public's visual space, and can be manifestations of a national/regional culture. Incentives must therefore be in place to promote the use of national and regional architectural styles as well as fashion (particularly clothing fashion of cultural significance).

The New Rules for a Functioning Market: Guardians of Transparency

Along with private property rights and an effective bureaucracy, transparency is paramount for the functioning of any economy. No matter how intelligent or well-intentioned a country's policies, laws, and regulations are, they cannot work if people can evade the law by paying off corrupt officials. The same principles apply to governance. No matter what system of government, it will never fulfil its intended goals if outside interests pay off lawmakers. If sound policy research determines a certain amount of spending is necessary, and large portions of that spending are siphoned off in corruption, then the policy is rendered ineffective.

In addition to a whole host of transparency laws, a fully independent, directly elected agency must be created to investigate corruption and to ensure the consistent application of law. This agency should have its own powers to arrest and prosecute, and should be modelled on successful anti-corruption agencies elsewhere (Romania and Singapore, for example). Guatemala has gone as far as to outsource the operation of their anticorruption agency to an international team, to ensure its independence. Considering the importance of transparency, it is not a surprise that a country goes this route. The New Physiocrats stipulate that such a highly independent and effective anticorruption agency must be in place before any other policy.

Unions in the public sector must be either outlawed or severely curtailed, as impediments to the democratic process. When the public wants an effective and efficient bureaucracy, free of corruption, the public must also be free to remove and replace employees. Public sector employees are already a voting bloc able to vote on their employment interests, which acts as a second layer of protection (in addition to unionization), which private sector employees do not have to the same extent. Unionized public sector employees also encourage governments to outsource public works to the private sector (as unionization tends to inflate costs), and these public-private partnerships can be more conducive to corruption.

Transparency should extend to the government's treatment of tax administration as well. Receipts for goods and services where taxes are applied should include a basic breakdown as to where those tax revenues are going. This can be applied to paystubs as well, where it can be shown that all income tax revenues are returned to income earners, via the NIS.

Private Property

Private property is the core element of any market-based economy. Without clear rules of ownership, strong private property rights, and a transparent, efficient, and predictable judiciary to enforce these rules, markets cannot function. Without property rights assigned (to land for example), nothing can be bought or sold, long-term investments cannot be made, taxes cannot be levied, and market prices cannot emerge. No policies or incentives can be effective without first ensuring secure property rights and an independent, trustworthy judiciary to administer them. The judiciary must also be free from political interference, follow due process, and be able to clear cases promptly. Finally, laws must be audited regularly to ensure they are streamlined, and to meet directives on efficient trials. This must be a constitutional right for business, in addition to protection against nationalization and direct intervention.

The Path to Full Employment

Since the development of modern macroeconomics, full employment was seen as a goal to be attained through monetary policy and aggregate demand. Some countries later recognized the role of labor market flexibility as well. However, even with supposedly cutting-edge monetary and demand management policies, the labor market still fails to clear. Economists overlook the roles played by lack of information, wage inflexibility, and not being able to adjust rapidly enough to changes in economic conditions due to slow retraining. The path to full employment means making sure the price of labor is appropriate to its supply and demand conditions. It also means ensuring the demand exists in the first place, and that the information exists to connect workers to employers. This requires the following steps:

- The most flexible possible labor market
    - Replacing the minimum wage and income taxation through the Three Pillars System; effectively subsidizing wages
    - Increasing citizens' purchasing power; further underwriting labor costs
    - Ease of relocation (downward pressure on housing costs and a preference for renting)
    - Limits on labor union power
    - Rapid, continuous retraining of the labor force
- Excellent transportation network that connects employees to employers
- A program to deliver market information about salaries, job availability, etc.
- Demand management through higher wages (Three Pillars System), and fiscal and monetary policy
- Correct the imbalance between peoples' working hours
- Create an employer of last resort for those deemed impossible to employ in the private sector at the time, utilized for public works

The Effort to Restore Our Time

Time, too, is something that can be monopolized, for those without choices of work or without a source of passive income. Typically, a person's time is exchanged for money, which is later exchanged for time again, when that money can be used for leisure or creativity. While work is necessary for our survival, it has been consuming a greater proportion of our time, despite our higher levels of productivity. Both work and time have been becoming increasingly skewed in their distribution, with some working longer hours, and others with no employment. Older workers sometimes avoid retirement, and are difficult to replace (or unable to retire), while younger workers remain unemployed or in low-level jobs. A lucky few have a balance between time and work, and are able to enjoy both a steady income and the privilege of time for leisure and creativity. For many types of work, longer hours also does not correlate with greater output, due to limits of the human body and mind.

The New Physiocrats recognize the importance of time, and its poor distribution. The New Physiocratic platform advocates an effort to value our time, and to reduce working hours in order to better distribute them, starting with a 30-hour work-week, plus a minimum of 30 vacation days per year. To discourage excess working hours (yet acknowledging it may be necessary at times), it would also require double pay for work in excess of 30 hours, and triple for excess of 40. Flexibility can be added to the rules by allowing a certain amount of time to be carried over to the following month, as long as overtime for all employees in a firm is capped (as a percentage of total working hours). Limits on store opening hours and days should also be removed, to further increase flexibility and adapt to people's preferences. Laws freeing employees' obligation to stay connected and receive messages outside of working hours, such as France's "right to disconnect" must be emulated. Non-compete clauses and no-poaching agreements must be restricted so workers are free to choose higher paying employers. Combined with the wage subsidy effect from the Three Pillars, flexible labor laws, and the other reforms in the Physiocratic platform, these reforms would become very affordable for both employers and employees. In contrast to the serious brain drain that countries such as South Korea have as a result of overwork, these policies would ensure the retention of top talent, rather than burning them out. It also allows more time for family and child care. In a further boost to the economy, it would allow time for entrepreneurial activities for those who desire them, yet don't have the time to pursue them.

The somewhat arbitrary nature of working hour regulations also means that they are by some measure a form of experimentation. Due to this reality, the working hour rules must be revisited every five years. A specific department, The Effort to Restore Our Time, should be tasked with collecting data on whether the above objectives are met for the nation and the individual, and to put forward policy proposals.

Bankruptcy

When an individual or corporation is unable to pay its debts, delaying bankruptcy or allowing it to become an overly long, drawn-out process, is just delaying the inevitable. While this might seem harmless, it in fact prevents resources from being properly allocated within the economy by delaying them from being sold off to new owners (who may be able to use them more efficiently). Bankruptcy also allows individuals and companies to shed debt, and return more quickly to their essential operations. There is real empirical evidence of this, particularly when comparing the economies of The Netherlands and Belgium, where Belgium recovered faster from the late-2000s recession (despite its more severe bureaucracy) with its significantly more streamlined bankruptcy processes.

The New Physiocratic platform, therefore, proposes time restrictions on bankruptcy cases, backed by significant judicial resources, bureaucratic simplification, and resources for affected employees. This ensures rapid readjustment and reallocation of resources when old businesses die out.

Perfect Information and Perverse Incentives: Publish salaries, education availability

The labor market fails due to gaps in information, along with a lack of capability to respond to the information that does flow through the market.

Before reaching adulthood, students are making important decisions about their place in the labor market. By their later years in schooling, they have typically selected their paths; either directly into the labor market, or into higher education such as university or college. At such a young age, most people are not yet aware what fields they might want to dedicate their life. Furthermore, the labor market conditions, salaries, and future career prospects are not well advertised for each field. Decisions made without this critical information leads to an underclass of graduates who are well educated but underemployed. Those who choose to re-educate themselves in a new field, face long, daunting, and sometimes expensive programs. The labor market takes an exceedingly long time to adjust and fill vacancies, or seeks imported labor.

To address this market failure, several policies need to be implemented. First, the government must publish a detailed list of salaries by job, sector, and geographic region, along with trends and prospects. It's not enough to host this information buried within the websites of national statistics agencies. Hard copies must be distributed to every household, informational boards must be posted in schools, and advertisements must be run with this information. It must also include information about living costs in each region, educational requirements, and where the relevant education can be obtained. Just as the prices for consumer goods are well known to the public, a concerted effort must be made to provide this labor market information. A new Department of Market Information must be tasked with such a job. Only then can people make informed decisions about their education and training. In addition, educational programs should be priced according to this market information, being free for areas that are most in demand.

Industry-Managed Rapid Retraining (IMRR)

Industry associations / Sectoral Banks must operate their own rapid training centers, offering focused training free of charge. By putting the education in the hands of the hiring industries themselves, the system can be used to quickly retrain workers and immediately place them into relevant jobs. While government-run education can be effective at providing a broad range of general skills, it is exceedingly slow to adapt, and to equip the labor force with specific, targeted skills. In short, the unemployed need to be encouraged to attend the retraining centers, and the employers need to assure their employment. With companies collectively having full control over the resources to do so, and being best placed to know what skills are needed, these training centers can be key tools to meet national targets on removing structural unemployment. When the Department of Labor Statistics detects unemployment due to a mismatch in skills, the following series of events would occur:

1. Wages in the affected sector will rise to attract the required labor due to market forces.
2. Effective dispersal of information across the country regarding the wage conditions.
3. The unemployed who are still receiving their income supplement, can only continue receiving it after a certain time frame, if they enrol in an accredited educational program (such as IMRR). This will increase pressure on the unemployed to enrol in retraining.
4. If for some reason the particular IMRR program is lacking capacity to train enough people to fill the vacancies, the relevant Sectoral Bank must report their reasoning and proposed solutions to the oversight commission.
5. Solutions will be implemented as requested by the Sectoral Bank (e.g., by adding more class space or teachers), conditional on the hiring of the said unemployed.

Employer of Last Resort

In the event that a citizen cannot find employment after retraining, and their National Income Supplement is ready to expire, they can visit the Department of National Restoration. This would function as an employer of last resort, in which the income supplement would be reinstated in exchange for taking an assigned part-time job. The mandate for this department would be to assign temporary jobs in areas where there is a labor shortage, and which would serve the nation and society. This could potentially include infrastructure building in remote regions, reforestation projects, cleaning public spaces, and environmental protection. The roles would be capped to a maximum contract length (e.g., 1 year) to encourage the workers' eventual reintegration into the private sector and to limit effects on market wages. The jobs would meet national labor regulations, and a certain amount of working time would be set aside for the workers to apply for permanent, private-sector work. Salaries would be equal to the NIS amount (in some cases in addition to provided housing). If more people lost employment in the private sector, the value of the NIS payment would automatically fall (as there would be fewer contributors), and would automatically discourage people from remaining in public employment, and shift labor resources back into the private sector.

This program would ensure that national labor resources do not go unutilized, and that the unemployed regain a sense of purpose and momentum. It would also avoid the trap of paying capable individuals to remain inactive. At the same time, it would not remove labor from the productive private sector. It would ensure full employment regardless of consumption growth. Finally, it would act as a backstop to prevent people from sliding into destitution, while filling needed vacancies to build the nation.

Freeing the Labor Market from its Distortions

Labor, like all other actors in a market, will produce a shortage or a surplus in the face of price controls. It is naïve to see how price controls on goods and services create artificial shortages and surpluses, and to think that labor would not be affected in the same way. Small companies are most negatively affected by minimum wage, given their more limited resources to hire. In a simple thought experiment, a minimum wage that's higher than the value that a worker is able to contribute, would result in very few companies able or willing to hire people. Some of the most extreme real-world examples were in American Samoa and Puerto Rico, which are under the jurisdiction of U.S. minimum wage laws, despite significantly lower productivity levels. The results in labor markets were catastrophic, and these U.S. territories faced mass layoffs, while protests ensued to be exempt from these wage laws. Automation has already been hastened by low skilled labor being under-priced by relatively cheaper capital. The solution is to subsidize labor (through the National Income Supplement program), to grant citizens a share in the national wealth, and to minimize the costs of essential goods; not to price workers out of the market.

With wages being bolstered with the National Income Supplement and the other pillars of income security, along with incentives to maintain executive pay ratios, unions must be freed to focus on other goals. While unions can form to ensure fair practices in the workplace, their influence on wages and corporate restructuring must be limited, to ensure competitiveness and that a free labor market is maintained. Unionization of government employees however, must be prohibited completely, to ensure there are no obstacles to democratic process, and that bureaucracy does not get in the way of the public's demands. Labor disputes must instead be dealt with through the CED in parliament (discussed below).

Burdensome regulations are another distortionary culprit for high rates of unemployment. Countries with inflexible regulations on hiring and firing are saddled with large numbers of unemployed. When it is difficult and expensive to hire employees, companies are hesitant to hire them in the first place. The same issue occurs with mandatory non-salary costs of employment. In addition, this lack of flexibility prevents workers from flowing out of dying industries, to where the labor market truly requires them. These costs must be minimized to promote employment, and labor regulations must instead focus on health and safety, working hours, and enforcement of labor contracts. Employees' financial security should instead be shouldered by the Three Pillars system of income support. Lessons can be learned from Denmark, which introduced its Flexicurity program in the 1990s, overhauling its labor market by maximizing flexibility, while protecting the unemployed and providing retraining; a program, which swiftly reduced long-term unemployment and advanced the Danish economy.

Sustainable Pensions and Savings

The current pension systems in much of the world were built to fail. They were created in a time of better age demographics, where a large, young labor force could easily support the small population of retirees. In many countries, the times have changed, and now a shrinking, aging workforce must support a large population of retirees. This imbalance means that workers pay an increasingly large share of their income to support retirees and are putting more into a bankrupt system that they might not get to enjoy.

The only solution that guarantees the security of pensions is to replace the system with individual pension and savings accounts, which we call, the Assisted Savings Program (ASP). But how do you ensure that lower and middle-income workers will have enough to retire on? How do you encourage saving? And how do you ensure that the majority of the population isn't forced to contribute unrealistic or objectionable amounts to their accounts?

Citizens would have mandatory, low contribution rates (e.g., 5% of net income after NIS and ND cash transfers), but have the option of increasing their contribution up to a maximum amount (20-40% of median income) — and would be rewarded generously for doing so. With the mandatory contribution including NIS and ND payments, it would guarantee that even those with spotty or no employment would be saving for their futures.

ASP contributions might also be deductible from income tax for 20-40% of median income, a deduction that would automatically change based on consumption, current-account metrics, and the unemployment rate. This would amplify the countercyclical effects of monetary policy, while still maintaining a large buffer of private savings.

All capital gains taxes (which would be taxed progressively, based on a person's income), must be redistributed to the ASP accounts. The funds raised would be distributed so that contributions are supplemented progressively, with contributions up to a certain percentage of the national median income receiving the largest supplements. For example, in a country where the median income is 30,000, contributions of up to the first 9,000 per year would receive the largest share of the savings supplement (the funds of which would be mostly derived from the capital gains taxes). Capital gains tax rates would be based on both personal income tax rate and length of time invested. For short-term investments, this would mean a capital gains tax rate equivalent to the investor's income tax rate. Investments of over 5 years in duration would be taxed at half the personal income tax rate (4% for low-income brackets, and 12% for high income brackets). Tax rates on investments for any duration between 0-5 years would be prorated. Capital gains as a result of high frequency trades (trades conducted within 10 seconds of one another) would be taxed at a higher rate of 32% (the revenues of which would also be distributed back to people's ASP accounts), so that all investors can enjoy the benefits of these trades, which they likely do not have the capability of performing themselves. Gains from passive income investment vehicles (such as passively managed ETFs and index funds) would face a 1-4% surtax (based on income), to ensure that invested funds are allocated efficiently, to deserving market performers. Using a progressive rate, along with the fact that these revenues are directed to ASP accounts, limits negative externalities for lower income earners with limited investment knowledge. Capital gains on property would not be taxed at all, as it would be earned income from improvements (as the ULT would tax the unearned income), and keeping in mind the aim to ensure the ease of transferring land to the best possible user. All of these capital gains tax revenues would be redistributed back to the market via individuals' ASP accounts. The account top-ups received would not be taxed at all, except for the capital gains, which grow from them.

People must be free to withdraw from these accounts early. The portion of saving contributions (plus the earned interest and redistributions) should be allowed to be withdrawn after 5 years of being deposited in the account, with a sizeable tax penalty. Early withdrawals after more than 5 years should be possible to withdraw with a decreasing tax penalty. Tax revenues collected from these early withdrawals should also be directed back into the pool, to be distributed back to the other accounts.

By distributing these capital gains/transaction taxes back into the financial markets or savings via ASP accounts, it would also ensure that no money is sucked out of the financial markets via taxation as it currently is, and would therefore be less distortionary. It would also redistribute short-term gains to invest in long-term investments. Finally, the program would also act to further supplement incomes and encourage long-term savings, rather than being strictly a pension program, and would serve to even out the incomes of people with less stable employment. In addition, there would be no demographic or financial risks that plague many developed nations with pay-as-you-go public pension programs.

The New Rules for Trade: Protectionism vs. Compensatism

The benefits of free trade are well known. In an ideal world, it allows countries to specialize in their strengths, promotes competition, ensures businesses can increase their scale and efficiency, lowers prices, and maximizes consumer choice. However, in practice, free trade is not as free as it might seem. The majority of countries subsidize their exports, protect their domestic markets through non-tariff barriers, manipulate their currencies' value, overlook environmental/labor standards, use state-controlled banks to provide subsidized lending, and subsidize inputs. By allowing these goods to flow across borders unfettered, the world ends up with far fewer competitors and market entrants than it should have, with only the most subsidized ones remaining. This means less consumer choice, and incumbents that can exercise excess pricing power over the market. In this situation, countries also don't get the opportunity to discover where their strengths are and what economic specializations they're best suited for. How can a country know if it's in a practical position to be the most efficient steel producer, if no new steel mills can survive in the face of the immense quantities of subsidized Chinese steel dumped onto the market? When governments decide to restrict the export of some of the more essential products (as China has done with rare metals), the dangerous reliance on importing them is exposed.

For free trade to work, labor must also be allowed to work freely in the participating countries. As countries focus on their specializations, their labor market becomes increasingly reliant on those specific industries they specialize in. This also sets them up for wrenching adjustments in the labor market, as the winds of demand can change from time to time. If labor cannot flow between the countries, which are freely trading with each other, people cannot follow these jobs as the changes occur, and many will be left without employment. Free movement of labor is also not realistic between all countries (due to preferences of the population, democratic demands, and culture), and therefore free trade is not always realistic either. When trade is free, but movement of labor is not, it results in countries specializing in a very narrow range of industries, and a labor pool that is completely reliant on them. When those industries start to fade, the population is hit hard. Diversification provides protection against risks, and a greater range of opportunities when a rising tide lifts other industries. While trade deals can be very valuable, the freest trade should occur between countries which are culturally similar and whose governments and companies play by the same rules.

Specialization can be a positive when the goods and services that a country specializes in are doing well in the market. However, if a country is specializing in areas that are more volatile, this can lead to tremendously destabilizing booms and busts. This is particularly the case with countries that are rich in natural resources, such as oil. When the price of oil is high, oil-rich countries see the benefits of their specialization, and their resources start to revolve around this sector. It is the most efficient way for the economy to maximize its output at that particular moment, and economic diversification becomes an afterthought. It is only when the price of the resource inevitably plummets when diversification seems like it would have been a good idea in hindsight. The labor market can take an exceedingly long time to readjust to the new economic reality.

A country cannot find its comparative advantage unless it is given the opportunity to try (and potentially fail) in a variety of sectors (e.g., South Korea with support for its ship-building industry). This is especially valuable to consider for a country in its earlier stages of development. A country might already have a comparative advantage in an area, but it might have difficulty getting it off the ground due to the behavior of incumbents.

If a country decides that it is harmful, for example, to pollute in excess, it can choose to put in place laws (or taxes) to minimize it. The producers in that country are then at a disadvantage compared to foreign competitors which are not burdened by these rules. If the country allows imports from these competitors, without compensating for the burden that the domestic producers have, then the domestic companies will be unable to compete, and possibly fail. Meanwhile, the country will also fail to reduce pollution, as they will be importing the goods from the polluting country without penalty. Producers can face similar artificial disadvantages in other situations, for example, if a particular currency zone happens to be over an area rich in a natural resource, and the price of that resource rises steeply and suddenly. While this is likely to be a temporary scenario, the strengthening of the currency as a result of changes in the current account balance may put other sectors out of business. When the price of the resource falls again, the economy is left with neither resource revenues, nor alternative sources of growth. The fact that a particular currency zone encompasses a region with this resource, was an artificial, man-made factor. With a tariff rate of 0, there is no compensation for these unfair, man-made disadvantages, and industries often fail due to these situations. In this case, it is difficult for a country to discover its natural specializations and strengths, and industries of particular national importance fail to materialize. With tariff rates too high, the opposite problem occurs. Countries are encouraged to produce goods they are ill-suited for, at high cost, gross inefficiency, waste, and with no little competitive pressure to reform.

When countries do decide to import goods and services from a subsidized origin, consumers do often benefit, at least initially, from low prices. Meanwhile, countries deciding to protect their industries from foreign competition are sometimes left with inefficient, uncompetitive industries, and consumers are burdened with the costs of higher prices. How can a country protect itself from the negative impacts of trade, while still enjoying its benefits? Both extremes can result in fewer competitive players, economic distortions, and unfair behavior that are detrimental to trading partners who play by the rules. The New Rules of Trade reconcile the two sides, to ensure the maximum benefits of global competition, without the harms of an unfair playing field.

Countries with natural resources, while blessed in some regards, are also cursed by them in others. By the sheer chance of having resources in the land within their borders, their currencies can rise and fall in value on the whims of commodities markets. A typical scenario that continues to present itself involves oil-rich countries' economies increasingly revolving around this resource and failing to diversify. It also has the potential to create an overreliance on its revenues, as governments are tempted to dish out lavish subsidies and ignore an ineffective tax collection system, only to find themselves struggling when oil prices inevitably drop. High resource prices can dramatically strengthen the exporting country's currency, putting a heavy burden on other export industries, flooding the country's market with imports, and leaving domestic competitors struggling. Export tariffs on raw materials, just high enough to compensate for the economic instability, are essential. They must also be placed on goods deemed Basic Essentials (such as food), to ensure a true domestic price, reflecting local incomes and economic conditions.

Using tariffs (and other forms of trade protection) are often not completely effective, particularly in floating currency regimes. As import tariffs put upward pressure on the country's current account balance, the currency tends to strengthen accordingly, and counteracts the effect of the tariff. The case of export tariffs has the same effect, in reverse.

However, by funneling tariff revenues into the sectors they are supposed to serve, these revenues will lower their costs (thereby lowering the costs for consumers) and provide funding for these sectors. The greater the demand for imports, the more tariff revenues, and the more funding for domestic investment. Direct subsidies are more prone to corruption, political interference, and run the risk of creating an incentive for these sectors to stop producing and relying on this new source of revenue. By directing the money to the Sectoral Banks of the affected sectors, funding needs are met automatically and funds are automatically adjusted based on domestic demand. This is all without the need for excess government bureaucracy, political interference, or for any other entity to decide on the amounts that are transferred. An independent research body must set the tariff rates.

Countries/regions/customs unions should have at least a limited degree of self-reliance in Basic Essentials (food, water, and housing; and potentially energy, essential infrastructure production, and clothing). Doing so:

- Provides protection against price shocks for imports (e.g., oil crises) and currency swings
- Means there is always a baseline demand for these products, as opposed to fast changing sectors affected by technology
- Can create domestic market prices that are different from world market prices, to spin off other industries (e.g., France's cheap electricity due to an abundance of nuclear energy)
- Realizes the strategic / security value of self sufficiency
- Recognizes that the increasing speed of creative destruction, reallocation of resources (especially labor) might be more costly than the inefficiency of not allowing pure comparative advantage (e.g., retraining older workers)
- Prevents complete hollowing out of industry as a result unfair trade, and Dutch disease
- Can be more true to comparative advantage, because it compensates for unfair trade, the arbitrary aspects of a nation / currency union's borders
- Acknowledges that country's propensity to be less diversified may be due to pure luck (natural resources) etc.
- Accepts that there will naturally be a certain class of people on the cutting edge who can easily switch jobs, and a certain class who can't — retraining is ideal but has its limits.
- Can be combined with free-trade zones where companies can take their varied skills and expose them to tougher competitive conditions.

Rules:

- Set the majority of import tariff rates at a level that only compensates for unfair practices and differences in regulations, set by an independent body

- Extra protection for Static Sectors
- Export tariffs on raw materials and Basic Essentials
- X years of protective consumption tariffs for developing countries
- Directing tariff revenues into Sectoral Banks
- Temporarily applied, gradually reducing protectionist tariffs for undeveloped countries
- Government initiation of Basic Essentials industries with a rapid timeline to privatize them

Preferential Trade Agreements

Preferential Trade Agreements would differ from free trade agreements, in that they would not aim for a zero tariff rate (except in the case of federations, customs unions, areas of free labor movement, or similar bodies). Instead, there would be greatly preferential tariff rates for countries under equivalent Physiocratic regimes, and moderately preferential rates for trade with countries handling trade in a fair manner.

Planned Obsolescence

Planned obsolescence is often a result of imperfect information in the market for consumer (and sometimes capital) goods. While companies provide specifications about their products, the only indicator of a product's lifespan is typically its warranty. Products are often produced to be irreparable, and information about repair-ability is typically opaque. Under the New Physiocratic platform, this lack of information is considered detrimental to the market's efficiency. In addition, we want to return to a time when products were built to last, constructed out of quality materials that felt tough, and could be repaired. To do so, the New Physiocratic platform calls for a series of laws like the Hamon Law introduced in France, which makes planned obsolescence illegal. It also would include strict labelling laws to indicate the expected length of a product's life, and availability of replacement parts. Products that cannot be repaired or upgraded must be labelled as such. A lean but effective agency would be tasked with the role of detecting such misbehavior, exposing quality control issues, and suggesting measures to increase durability. The levels and grades of durability would also be rated on an easy-to-read scale (for example, a 1 for a product that is fragile, and a 10 for a product that can be battered with no effect). The agency would also distribute consumer quality awards, perhaps even televised for entertainment, where products are put to the durability test. The New Physiocrats believe in a return to the days of products that were built to last, and if consumers prefer a more fragile product, they should at least be informed before purchasing.

Economic Complexity

The more diversity in a country or region's economy and the greater the range of skills and experience, the more able the place is to find new pathways of growth. The modern-day emphasis on specialization, while beneficial when this specialization is in demand, seems misguided at the times when it is not. The New Physiocrats believe that too much emphasis on specialization can result in more intense boom and bust cycles, with too little protection against downside risks. Where there are a diverse range of skills and industries, an economy can reorient itself to other areas where there may be a higher payoff, meaning more stability, and higher capacity for continued advancement. We refer to this potential for a wider range of growth pathways as Economic Capacity. After observing these patterns independently, the New Physiocrats discovered the Economic Complexity Index, developed by economists at MIT. While their model may have different roots, they too use economic complexity (diversity) as predictive indicator for economic growth, and founded The Observatory of Economic Complexity.

Chilean-style capital controls

A floating, yet stable, market-determined exchange rate, that reflects the long-term balance of a country's current account is the only sustainable currency regime. Heavy-handed interventions in forex markets will always result in domestic imbalances eventually. Time after time, we see artificially overvalued currencies collapse, inflicting tremendous pain on consumers as they face a shock to their purchasing power. This has happened repeatedly in countries with pegged or managed exchange rate regimes and open capital accounts.

Artificially undervalued currencies come with their own set of problems; in particular, overreliance on exports and a severe misallocation of resources as seen in countries such as China, as well as tensions with trading partners. The beauty of a floating currency is that it acts as an automatic stabilizer to the domestic economy. If net exports are reduced, a floating currency weakens, automatically rebalancing the balance of trade. It stimulates or dampens the domestic economy as needed, and helps to manage inflation.

The exception to this rule is when large speculative inflows come into the picture. In certain global financial conditions, short-term, speculative capital can flood economies with funds to reap quick rewards; this is referred to as hot money. It can quickly strengthen the currency of the country it enters, rendering the country's exports uncompetitive. It can also leave just as quickly as it entered, causing tremendous destabilization to the country's domestic market and currency valuation. Taking emergency measures to stem the outflow of capital is rarely effective in these crises; the capital controls are always evaded, and tend to create opportunities for corruption. This was the story of the Asian Financial Crisis of the 1990s, as well as the Russian and Argentine financial crises, among others.

The remedy to this issue lies in a method Chile experimented with in the 1990s. Speculative inflows were limited through a tax on short-term inflows (mainly through a non-remunerated reserve requirement on foreign liabilities). This effectively changed the composition of inflows (to be tilted toward longer-term investment) without reducing inflows overall, and protected Chile from the effects of hot money. The Chilean peso maintained its stability, and the domestic economy was insulated from the financial shocks that affected many other emerging markets during this decade. The New Physiocrats strongly endorse this policy of a floating currency combined with taxing short-term inflows. To mitigate the potential effects of making capital more expensive, under our platform, the revenues raised would be split between ASP accounts and Sectoral Banks, balancing incentives for equity and debt financing.

The New Rules on Government Spending

There is no end to the upward creep in government spending as a percentage of GDP. For most countries, the ratio of government spending to the total size of the economy has been consistently on the rise since the Great Depression. The problem with this in itself, is that it creates a heavier and heavier burden for the wealth producing private sector to shoulder. Also, without any checks on spending, politicians often spend heavily before elections. Politicians rarely even show restraint on spending when the economy is growing, leaving budgets with dangerously little cushioning for when the economy slows down. The massive increase in national debt burdens since the late-2000s recession could have been prevented, even with deficit spending, had countries been running larger surpluses during the years of economic growth. Instead, countries are left with less fiscal firepower with each passing recession, and with greater debt burdens for future generations to pay off.

While some might propose dangerous, radical solutions, such as monetizing debt (which punishes individuals who were prudent enough to save), the truth is that you cannot make money out of thin air. Fiscal conservatism with appropriate rules-based spending is necessary — without question — to prevent economic and financial crises. While they are two resource-rich countries facing an array of similar issues, comparing the fiscal conservatism of Bolivia, versus the fiscal profligacy of Venezuela and the outcomes are a damning testimony to a lack of fiscal discipline.

Constitutional fiscal rules would prompt governments to take a hard look at spending priorities, and run cost-benefit analyses when making spending decisions. Learning from the mistakes of others, the New Physiocrats are firmly in favor of strict spending discipline, preferring only to use deficit spending as a means to rapidly implement the platform in its initial years, and during unexpected emergencies. Fiscal stimulus on a national level is now often lost due to leakage, as economies are typically not as closed as they were during the years of Keynes, and act as a short-term band-aid solution at the expense of future growth. It does not address structural issues. In particular, countries running trade and current account deficits need to explore whether this is due to supply side and competitiveness issues, as these are indicators of countries consuming more than they are producing. Using fiscal stimulus to kick-start consumer demand can often be self-defeating in these cases, as the funds are spent on imports.

Constitutional provisions must be made to limit total spending as a percentage of GDP, to prevent adjustments in spending in an election year, and to ensure surpluses are maintained during years of growth. Only then will government budgets stop amplifying boom-bust cycles, stop encouraging corrupt practices, and begin to chip away at waste and excess.

Focus on Incentives

We divide government spending into two main categories: cash compensation and general spending. Cash compensation consists of the cash payments to citizen-residents (paid via the National Dividend, National Income Supplement, and Assisted Savings Program), and to businesses (via the Sectoral Banks). General spending consists of the remainder of government spending. For the correct Physiocratic incentives to be in place, all general spending must come solely from the ULT and the SVAT. Even building taxes (part of the ULT) must be returned to the population as cash compensation, so as both to compensate the public, and to ensure the government is not incentivized to promote inappropriate buildings. By relying on the ULT (whose revenues are split between the national and regional governments), the incentives would be aligned for governments to develop infrastructure, educational facilities, workplaces, and beautiful spaces, as these would raise land values (thereby further raising tax revenues). A reliance on the SVAT incentivizes the government to promote rises in median incomes, as sustainable, rising consumption growth would be the only way to raise revenues from this source.

Part III: Political Reform Platform

A New System of Government

There will always be conflicting interests in society, and therefore in government. Every interest group has a voice, but in different (figurative) volumes, depending on their financial clout and political connections. It is important for many of these groups to have a voice, because without one, governments can inadvertently make decisions that cause them harm. The problem is in the way these groups make their voices heard.

A typical example is when a nation's parliament is preparing to vote on a particular issue that will affect several facets of society or the economy. Certain segments form lobby groups (or rally their existing lobby groups) to petition the government to influence the decision. Although the reasons for doing so might be important, for example preventing undue harm to their industry, the means often take the form of corruption. These processes of lobbying and corruption also mean that some industries or interests have an unfair share of the national voice. Many interest groups have no voice at all. It also creates an environment where conflicting interests are fighting for opposing measures and bog down government progress.

Instead, a system of government must be created where the public produces a blueprint for the direction of the country, and can organize the society's and economy's interest groups to work for them. These interest groups should then be able to share the national forum to discuss their needs and concerns in an absolutely transparent manner, in plain view of the public.

In effect, the public would be presenting their goals, and then the nation's interest groups would organize to meet them. The interest groups would propose the requirements that they would need to meet the nation's goals, and thrive with their own operations, in a grand reconciliation process.

This system would bring lobbying, currently an avenue for corruption, into a channel for all individuals and sectors to voice their needs with complete transparency. The reconciliation process would create a powerful means in which to organize the nation's resources to meet the needs of the public, by making the (often conflicting) parts of society work together harmoniously.

Concurrently, the constitution must include rules based on Ireland's Lobbying Act, an exemplary rule set to ensure the utmost transparency in lobbying, with a special body to oversee these rules. It uses the broadest possible definition of a lobbyist, defined as "anyone who employs more than 10 individuals, works for an advocacy body, is a professional paid by a client to communicate on someone else's behalf or is communicating about land development is required to register themselves and the lobbying activities they carry out."

To implement such a system, while maintaining the values of the New Physiocrats, a quadricameral parliament must be in place. It would comprise the following 4 chambers:

> The Chamber of National Objectives (CNO)
> The Chamber of Economic Design (CED)
> The Chamber of National Society (CNS)
> The Chamber of Transparency (COT)

The Chamber of National Objectives (CNO) must consist of directly elected representatives, using ranked ballots with a single transferable vote (STV) method, and an independent districting organization (to prevent gerrymandering). It must also have a Swiss-style direct democracy component, in which the public can introduce bills to the chamber. Each district must be relatively large to reduce corruption (by being answerable to a large number of people), and to increase government efficiency and expense (reduce the number of local governments).

The chamber would be responsible for drafting a long-term (10-year) vision; one that would be representative of the desires of the population. This would be the starting point from which the entire legislature would work together to plan its course of action.

The purpose of the Chamber of Economic Design (CED) would be to draft forward-looking economic policies based on the CNO's vision. The chamber would be divided into two halves: producers and consumers. The producer half would be subdivided into the three original factors of production, land, labor, and capital. Ensuring that the needs of producers and consumers are met equally would guarantee growth in production, balanced by the needs, safety, and health of the markets they sell to, and without large current account imbalances.

The capital division of the CED must assemble capital industry groups together by their respective Sectoral Banks. This would include seats for the Basic Essentials Bank, Agriculture Bank, Manufacturing Bank, Resource Exploration Bank, Strategic Technology Bank, Infrastructure Industry Bank, Electrical Energy Bank, Export Development Bank, National Defense Bank, Housing Bank, Cultural Bank, and the Startup Bank. Each of these divisions would be of equal size, and would be elected by companies in their respective industries.

The land division of the CED would consist of three directly democratically elected organizations: the Ministry of Environment, the Ministry of Visual Space, and the Renters Union. These would represent all the interests of locations and physical space, including the environment, architecture / other elements of visual space, and accessibility of space for living.

The labor division would consist of unions and other labor organizations. The formation of these organizations would be very simple, as would be their ability to enter the chamber. Yet the powers to directly negotiate employer-paid wages and cash equivalents would be unavailable, as this goes against the principles of price-wage flexibility of the New Physiocrats, which recognize the incredible damage of price and wage controls. Instead, their role in government would be to formulate sound policy for the labor market in all other areas they see fit, and to address the labor markets concerns. This would include working hours, granting the labor market a degree of democratic control over their own time (working hours). If an employee is not already a member of a labor organization, they would be assigned a government-created one representing labor in a broad economic sector (mirroring the Sectoral Banks; e.g., a manufacturers' union), from which they would be free to switch.

The consumers half of the CED would consist of organizations related to end consumers, chiefly the democratically elected Department of Consumer Protection, and the Consumers Bank. The interests of these groups would be aligned with consumer safety, fairness, prices, and product quality/longevity.

Each half of the CED would have an equal number of seats, and each division within the halves would also have an equal number of seats. By balancing the powers of consumers, producers, labor, and physical space; cartel-like behavior would be mitigated, while offering a forum for all voices to be heard.

Not only would the CED give citizens a measure of control over their economic future (within the context of a free market), it also grants the public a tool to protect national interests in the face of competing countries that use state-run entities to achieve their geopolitical objectives. Economic groups would have a channel to raise concerns about unfair practices, and agree on a course of action with all other segments of the economy and society.

The Chamber of National Society (CNS) would also be divided into two halves: Urban and Rural, each with an equal number of seats. This chamber would be purposed with ensuring that the cultural, social, and economic interests of each societal group are voiced. There must be reserved divisions for the democratically elected departments for urban and rural affairs, elected by urban and rural voters respectively. The remaining seats would be filled by regional, ethnocultural, and arts groups based on population, which would be freely formed by members of the public. Depending on where the group originates and where its activities and members reside, would determine which half of the chamber in which it would be placed. Publicly owned media could even be divided along urban-rural lines, to further advance the representation and views of both sides.

The purpose of the Chamber of Transparency (COT) must be to preserve government transparency, present a cost-benefit analysis on spending/regulatory bills, guarantee that the long-term interests of the country are ensured, and that the articles of the constitution are abided by. The chamber would consist of the independently elected Ministry of Transparency & Efficiency (MTE), the League of Futurists & Historians (LFH), and the Constitutional Guard.

The MTE would have the power to monitor, record, and broadcast parliamentary actions through its own media services. It would have to answer to any public concerns about corruption, and its compensation structure would be a function of the public score on corruption.

Impeachment of its members would be possible via public petition. It would operate the national anti-corruption agency, meaning this agency would also answer to public demands. Finally, this would be the division responsible for presenting the cost-benefit analysis on spending/regulatory bills.

The LFH would be elected on longer (10-year) terms, and would require special qualifications to run for election. Half of the members must be under 40 years old, and all members must carry certain high-level qualifications in history and economic history. Salaries would be particularly high, and a function of median net income (adjusted for purchasing power) and environmental and social indicators. Its role would be to provide a long-term, far-forward-looking decision-making arm in government, and to compare policies to those previously applied in foreign countries as well as domestically. In part, it would inform government on the long-term effects of its proposed policy decisions, and recommend alternative options. As with other positions, members could be impeached by public petition.

The Constitutional Guard would be elected by the members of the Constitutional Law Guild, which in itself would have special educational requirements in constitutional law and New Physiocratic principles for its licenses.

While the Chamber of Transparency could not introduce new bills, it would closely monitor the actions of parliament, present any concerns, and a supermajority majority vote in the chamber would have the power to veto any bills, regardless of origin. The public must also retain the ability to petition the leadership of the anticorruption agencies and sections of the COT to step down if there is overwhelming support for impeachment. The independence of the anticorruption framework is paramount to the sound implementation of policy.

Legislative bills could be introduced freely by any of the divisions, aside from the COT, as long as a division has its own majority in which to do so. The bills would then need to be voted on within the entire chamber, reconciled, and approved by a majority in each chamber.

Presidents would be elected to 5-year terms and would be judged by their ability to work toward the public's 10-year visions in the face of unknown circumstances and potential shocks.

Financial and Monetary Reform

Time after time, in market economies, we have seen the economic cycle follow the credit cycle (which has trended toward being a function of the property market cycle). Credit expands, consumers and the private sector go into debt, fuelling a boom. If and when the debt becomes unsustainable, companies and consumers cut back on spending to repay their debts, and those who are unable to, go bankrupt. If this happens across the economy on a large enough scale, the economy can fall into recession, or worse. The policy response to mitigate recessions in these events, has been a combination of increased fiscal spending, and monetary stimulus (low interest rates, bond purchases, etc.). If governments have run a large enough fiscal surplus (if any) during the boom years, they may be able to fund the deficits without going into debt. However, since economies do not operate in a vacuum, and are sometimes exposed to surprises and external shocks, governments may sometimes decide they need to use debt to finance spending to fill gaps in aggregate demand. This creates an inverse relationship between private and public debt, which we see empirically. Additionally, central banks use a small toolset — mainly interest rates — to encourage lending over saving to further stimulate demand.

Since the end of the Second World War, many developed nations have seen their private debt levels (as a percentage of GDP) balloon to new heights. Up to a certain point, this private debt increase was a positive; invested into new businesses, industries, and technologies that fuelled a post-war boom. The credit was invested very effectively, in businesses which paid off, and debt was still at a level manageable enough to be repaid. Debt can be a positive force; it's just a matter of finding an ideal level. As time went on, private debt reached exceedingly high levels, with a rising share driven toward existing assets (as opposed to creating new assets), such as real estate. In addition to driving up living costs (due to inflated real estate markets), this also created systemic risk in the economy beyond issues related to mortgage-backed securities. As a result of these rising private debt levels, at the end of each credit cycle, the amount of debt being repaid keeps rising; resulting in more demand being sucked out of the economy. Thus, deflationary pressures build up, and policymakers react with ever lower interest rates, and ever higher public debt. The overall debt levels have continued to expand, but have also been shifting between the public and private sectors. Since the late-2000s recession, real economies have been unresponsive to the unprecedented levels of stimulus, while asset prices have soared. Governments then imposed budgetary austerity to attempt to control soaring public debt. The gap in demand was never completely closed, and governments and central banks proved incapable of closing it.

It is arguable where exactly the gap in demand lies, considering many of the same countries with slack in their labor markets also face large trade and current account deficits (which sounds more like a gap in domestic supply). However, efforts to combat deflation or disinflation are best met with demand-side measures. For the US in particular, the most recent challenges involved a combination of overly low inflation, persistent current account deficits, slack in the labor market, high levels of public and private debt, and an unusually slow recovery. Tackling these issues with low interest rates and quantitative easing has been an extremely inefficient way of attempting to support demand. While it was (too) successful in boosting demand for assets, it proved to be ineffective in increasing investment and propping up demand where it was needed. In addition, these policies only encouraged taking on further debt, setting up the economy for more risk in the future. The fiscal policy options are also poor, between taking on excess government debt (purchasing growth from the future), or spending cuts (further decreasing demand and growth). Raising inflation targets to cut debt can also cause serious harm. If done with the same policy tools as the central banks currently use, then in addition to reducing purchasing power, it would also worsen the already dangerous asset price bubbles.

The only viable solution to the current crisis is to monetize some of the current public debt and enforce spending within strict rules and limits. While it is a taboo topic, as long as it is done within a defined rule set, low inflation targets, and as a seldom-used emergency measure, it can be done safely and without creating perverse incentives. This contrasts with the dangers of negative interest rates, quantitative easing, and all other available options.

Some monetary reformists advocate full reserve banking, with a central bank that fully monetizes government expenses as a means to adjust the money supply. While a financial system completely reliant on oversized banks for monetary operations puts the economy in a precarious situation, so does a system entirely reliant on a centralized government authority, except in the latter case with even more perverse incentives, and a temptation to overinflate the economy. Others argue for the abolishment of central banks altogether, but this has the same effect, with power centralized in the hands of a few, and leaving the public without tools to handle crises. Money creation must instead be balanced between public and a diversity of private entities, with all of them paying fees to the citizens to compensate for the privilege.

To prevent the present-day monetary dilemmas in the future, central banks must also target ideal rates of private debt, and bank capital requirements should be kept at a range of 15-25%, as recommended by Lord Adair Turner (former chairman of the UK's Financial Services Authority). Controlling debt levels in the economy combined with ensuring high capital requirements (allowing movement within the 15-25% range, for countercyclical rules) are a far simpler alternative to defeat the systemic risk in the financial system. It can replace a whole host of complicated, expensive regulations, which anyway have holes torn in them by special interests. Similarly, minimum mortgage deposits should be around 25%, which would make property prices respond more accurately to demand, and encourage savings and investment. It also compensates for the disadvantages of housing ownership, such as anchoring the labor force to one location. Finding the ideal level of private debt in an economy is not so black and white; however somewhere within the extremes lies an ideal range that combines a sustainable rate of growth without an unacceptable level of risk. The tax benefits of debt (over equity) must also be removed, to discourage serious economic distortion. This may be done either through the taxation of debt, or by allowing deductions for the cost of equity, preferably through the latter. The regulatory costs of listing on an exchange and remaining there should also be considered as an artificial disincentive for raising money through equity, and tax credits should be issued for such expenses.

A levy on private money creation would further reduce systemic risk (modelled on the UK bank levy, except at a higher rate). Meanwhile, it would automatically reduce debt and inflation while promoting growth if these new revenues are distributed evenly between the National Dividend (reducing consumer debt), Sectoral Banks (reducing corporate debt while lowering prices), and local/national governments (reducing government debt or tax burdens) as lending grows. This creates a unique scenario where lending growth and private seigniorage growth may actually translate into reduced rates of inflation, as it would convert into expanded production of Basic Essentials (via the Sectoral Bank mechanism). With high capital requirements and the new levy, central banks might also require extra tools to meet their targets; yet these tools would also provide more diverse streams of liquidity.

Typically, when lending fuels growth, it also fuels inflation, as the money supply and velocity increase, yet production of the basic essential goods we rely on, do not increase in supply with it. Wages tend to chase prices, and it is difficult to get out of a price-wage inflationary (or deflationary) spiral. However, with the policy tools and automatic mechanisms in place to direct some of the flow of cash towards the production of Basic Essentials, and toward the National Dividend, the public is compensated for the externalities of increased lending (and monetary privileges), and ample funding for the production of Basic Essentials would keep price growth in check. A UK-style bank levy (on debts) at a rate of 0.3%, automatically distributed evenly three ways, between Sectoral Banks, the National Dividend, and general government revenues, would ensure that the benefits of people's labor are properly rewarded, without their wages lagging behind inflation. By offering central banks the possibility to also engage with these programs such as Sectoral Banks and the Three Pillars (within strict rules), these positive effects can be multiplied, and central banks would better achieve their targets without resorting to dangerous measures such as ultra-low rates and quantitative easing (QE).

On the consumer side, consumers need both protection against unethical behavior, and also to feel the consequences of their own banking decisions. An agency for consumer protection in the financial sector would be of benefit, especially in the realm of misleading behavior by lenders.

With regards to deposit insurance, the New Physiocrats recommend a regulation that ensures depositors must always have 10% of savings unprotected. This must be combined with rules enforcing extraordinarily transparent and visible advertising on the bank's key metrics for risk, reserve ratios, and failure scenarios, so that consumers can make informed decisions, and so that rigorous market discipline is enforced on banks.

New Central Bank Rules and Tools

- Strict long-term price level targeting (based on an average inflation rate of 2%)
- Targets to control asset price growth — particularly housing
- Allowances for deflation in Basic Essentials
- Private debt level targets
- Unemployment / underemployment rate targets
- Targeting a long-term balance between investment and consumption, as well as current accounts
- Power to offer monetary financing of public fiscal spending, within strict rules
- Power to offer monetary financing to Sectoral Banks, strictly to fund non-lending operations
- Monetary financing can only be offered after 2+ years of fiscal surpluses, with a limit on the number of consecutive years of monetary financing, and with a value limit as a percentage of GDP
- Power to provide cash top-ups for the Three Pillars Program, within strict conditions
- Power to raise minimum deposit amount for mortgages
- Power to manage and adjust the 15-25% bank capital requirement
- Power to bolster the tax rate and rules on short-term capital inflows
- Some additional regulatory powers over the financial system
- Rigorous restrictions on providing stimulus during critical political moments such as elections

Restricting monetary financing to specific areas such as infrastructure funding, public works, and Three Pillars funding, gives central banks very direct levers over unemployment rates and consumption demand, without the need for the colossal amount of QE and debt we see today (which are far more indirect ways of influencing unemployment). Of course, there must be restrictions on when these policies can be used in order to prevent abuse, corruption, and dangerous incentives. Restrictions on timing as well, to safeguard central bank independence from the political process, are also a necessary precursor to such a policy. By offering the possibility of monetary financing in addition to traditional sources of financing as source of growth, there are more options and policy tools to provide liquidity and stimulus in the event of emergency. Some of these tools should be used as a last resort, however they would be incredibly useful in the exceptional monetary conditions much of the world has faced since the late 2000s financial crisis.

Using price level targeting, as opposed to a pure inflation target, along with the other new powers we offer, would provide central banks with a potent toolkit to meet its new targets. At the same time, allowing a completely free-floating currency regime without any exchange rate targets, would free the central banks' resources to focus on these more important goals, and better allow the economy to adjust to shocks. Finally, by granting the central banks these extra tools, they will not be forced to overuse dangerous levers such as interest rates and quantitative easing, thereby allowing interest rates to be determined more naturally.

The New Physiocrats' platform uses tax incentives to ensure long-term thinking in financial markets, so that directors and shareholders are invested in the future of their companies, to compensate the public for high frequency trading methods that most people do not have access to, and to encourage rational decision-making over accidental or emotional market moves. However, the New Physiocrats are also against pure financial transactions taxes. While trying to limit volatility and avoid sudden drops, these taxes instead encourage fewer but much larger, and potentially more catastrophic, market moves. In addition, by limiting financial taxes to profits and capital gains, the entire population can benefit from these returns, especially with the advent of the New Physiocrats' proposal for ASP accounts.

This is a financial and monetary plan that seeks to increase safety by creating self-reliant, separated financial institutions, which cannot cause cascading collapse. It creates a wide array of policy options, to diversify solutions in response to unknown future shocks, while not needing to predict them. These strategies replace a whole host of complex regulations, and the loopholes and unexpected outcomes that come with them. It uses the simplest possible solutions, such as significantly increasing capital requirements, a reversal of policies encouraging excessive debt, a separation of commercial and investment banking, and abandoning QE and low rates. With these policies in place, other financial regulations could be scaled back dramatically, corporate financial reporting could be reduced to biannually, and central banks would be empowered with new stimulus options that don't run up private or national debts.

Part IV: Social Reform Platform

Culture and Free Speech

The New Physiocrats believe in the same standards for freedom in the space of communications as we do for physical space, in that it should be accessible to all. The New Physiocrats are resolutely in favor of free speech and communication of ideas without any restrictions whatsoever, believing this to be one of the core principles of the most successful societies. Free speech protections would be extended to all public spaces, including universities, where in recent years these protections have particularly eroded.

The same principles must be applied to the internet and to media, where the New Physiocrats endorse a South Korean model of net neutrality. Local and regional content requirements might be beneficial as a means of promoting more diverse media while preserving culture. As would a variety of publicly funded media channels representing each region in addition to channels to specifically deliver separate urban and rural content. Anti-trust laws in media must be enforced with importance in mind.

Marriage and Child-rearing

The topic of marriage in much of the Western world has been focused on who should be able to get married. As the New Physiocrats, taking inspiration from, nature and the ecosystem, we believe this should be left up to the individuals involved to decide, and for nature to run its course. Just as with businesses in a free market with perfect information, any two partners (regardless of gender) who come together and decide to get married, should be allowed to do so, and rise or fall under the merits of the arrangement. We do note, however, that just as information isn't perfectly available in the market for goods and services, it is also imperfect in the market for finding a partner.

However, with divorce rates exceptionally high, birth rates exceptionally low, and the corruption of family law, we also see something rotten in the institution of marriage, which we see in urgent need of reform. We see mistrust between partners, financial difficulties, financial incentives for divorce, lack of bonding, the sacrifice of family for career, late-age births, short-term thinking, lack of partner interdependence, society undervaluing parenthood, lack of income and income stability, lack of time, urbanization, lack of living space, and marriage decisions being made without adequate information about partners, as being contributing factors to the failure of marriage. Divorce must also be seen through a lens of economic incentives, as spousal support payments in their various forms, function as a redistribution of income. With divorce rates hovering around 50% in the developed world, it can be a tremendous distortion in work incentives, affecting a large segment of the population. The tax of spousal support should instead be replaced with the Three Pillars of economic support. Perhaps we should take some time to reflect on the purpose of marriage and the goals it was meant to achieve.

Marriage (consisting of two-parent households) has long been the foundation for producing healthy productive members of society in adequate numbers, and with the right education and attributes. In the developed world, it has done so quite successfully until recently. The stable, two-parent household model is still an ideal to reaching these goals, yet publicly funded daycare, handouts, and tax breaks for parents have proven inadequate to sufficiently boost birth rates. The New Physiocrats offer the following policy prescription:

- Introduce a marriage phase-in period; the first 22 months of marriage would consist of a period of cohabitation, followed by an 8-week separation period. The marriage could be dissolved without divorce at any point during these periods, and the marriage process would only be complete after completing both phases.
- Ending no-fault divorce after the phase-in period
- Extending National Income Supplement for a stay-at-home parent in a married family
- Large increase in available leisure time through the Effort to Restore Our Time

- Reform of divorce courts to remove corruption, perverse financial incentives, and poor outcomes for children
- Define the principal goal of marriage to be the rearing of healthy children
- Raise the cultural status of child-rearing and family life

Introducing a phase-in period for marriage would ensure that both partners have the appropriate information they need to decide whether to continue with the marriage. It would reduce the rate of a marriage market failure, by removing risk during a period with a lack of information, or information clouded by emotion. It would also bring more young people into the fold of marriage, making it less risky to marry during a time of significant life changes.

After the phase-in period, marriage would become much more permanent, with more asset fusion, and without the possibility of no-fault divorce; thereby providing assurances for the married partners, and encouraging them to work through any difficulties they may face. Grounds for divorce would remain conventional (abuse, adultery, desertion, addiction, imprisonment, alienation, lack of intimacy, etc.).

In many places, divorce courts have become an avenue for corruption to enrich lawyers (and sometimes judges), pitting parents against each other, all to the detriment of the children. Just as the principal goal of marriage would be child-rearing under the Physiocratic platform, the interests of the children would be placed as a top priority in the event of divorce, including 50-50 custody. Only publicly employed lawyers should be used in divorce proceedings, and perhaps the use of a jury as well. The removal of alimony would eliminate excess involvement of cash in the divorce process.

If the partner then decides to become a homemaker after the phase-in period, they would be entitled to 50% of the full NIS payment. The payment would rise to 75% after one child, and 100% after two children. A parent should never have to decide between taking care of their children (while furthering their spouse's career success) and their own financial independence or entrepreneurial desires.

As those who are employed outside the home would also receive the NIS payments, parents would not be penalized for deciding between returning to other lines of work; parents would have complete liberty over their decisions. Furthermore, empowering people with these options would provide much competition to daycare providers, and help keep a lid on their prices.

The NIS payments would also raise the status of child-rearing as an occupation, especially when combined with a public media campaign to emphasize the value of the occupation. A Minister of Demography would be assigned with the task (among others) of facilitating such a cultural change, through promotions and competitions.

NIS payments would also serve as a replacement for alimony in the event of a divorce. NIS payments would be maintained after the marriage for the same length of time (and under the same rules) as the marriage was in effect. This would maintain income stability without labor market distortions, and would prevent unnecessary suffering. In addition, it would grant homemakers much more independence, or subsidize their transition into retraining or into new lines of work.

Child-rearing must be recognized as a true occupation, not only due to the work involved, but also due to the importance of preparing the next generation for the future. It also has a Ricardian element of economic specialization, where if one parent is focused on child-rearing, it allows the other parent to maximize their focus on growing the family income. This would cause available funds for the NIS to automatically rise even more. Finally, there is a certain unfairness in the current system, where being a nanny is recognized as a profession (as it pays a salary), while a homemaker is not, despite providing equivalent or better utility.

Additional measures such as further financial incentives to meet demographic targets might be required in some cases, but culture plays an increasing role as well. By ensuring more equal political-economic influence to rural areas (which tend to have higher birth rates) to stem the rural-urban exodus, the New Physiocratic governing system may aid in this regard as well. As would the ULT policies to maximize the amount of affordable living space. However, a ministry tasked with resolving demographic issues may also require cultural tools such as a media presence to offer more positive voices promoting family life over conspicuous consumption.

The combination of the marriage reform as outlined, with dramatic increases in incomes and free time as a result of the other New Physiocratic policies, would restore marriage as an institution, and better the lives of all participants. The improved funding mechanisms for rural regions (including the Agricultural Bank) and 50-50 sharing of rural-urban parliamentary representation would support the regions that are the biggest contributors to birthrates. Meanwhile, with living space better distributed and utilized, those concerns would be allayed as well. It would also address information gaps in the marriage market and remove the elements of corruption and perverse incentives which plague marriage today.

Reproductive rights must be maintained for women, while the playing field must also be equalized for men. This may mean a bill of procreative rights to ensure equality, in which women are guaranteed rights to their reproduction, while men are not penalized for decisions outside of their control. It may also mean automatic paternity testing upon birth. This would not only ensure fairness and responsibility, but lessen risks for entering marriage contracts, resulting in further benefits to this demographic program.

Immigration policy must use a points system centered on economic and cultural fit. It must also be disconnected from population growth rate targets, so it does not become a crutch to deal with domestic demographic issues. This would ensure that immigrants who arrive are those who are desired as opposed to being a means to plug governments' fiscal gaps or inflate economic growth figures. As with relying on imports for other essential inputs for production, an overreliance on imported labor can put a country at risk. This must be balanced by taking into account the benefits that immigrants can bring, as well as humanitarian concerns.

Implemented in their entirety, these reforms would address issues of fairness while ensuring control over physical space through a demographic lens.

Our Space and Health

Health and disease control are a matter of public space, and the effects of disease, obesity, and health are felt and seen by all. Governments in a New Physiocratic system therefore have a mandate of maintaining public health, as much as they do space. While personal choices and freedoms are paramount, taxation (on sugars for example), must be incorporated into the platform to compensate the public for this behavior. All citizens must be insured by a public health system, using the best frameworks and practices (as measured by results; e.g., France, etc.) while choices must be maximized with public and private systems operating concurrently.

Our Space and Education

A lack of school choice traps children in the neighborhoods they were born into, with the same social environment, for the duration of their education. Essentially this limits their freedom of movement, both physically as well as in terms of social mobility. Students cannot associate with people from outside their neighborhoods and economic status, and are stuck in their assigned school. This is against the very essence of the New Physiocrats and the movements that preceded it, which went to great lengths to advocate freedom of location and shared public space. Public education must therefore change to a voucher system, where public schools have flexibility over how they operate, and where funds are tied to the student, in addition to just the schools themselves, so that students can choose a school in any district. Education without a voucher system is a monopoly, and comes with the harmful effects that come with all monopolies. Students and families must be free to pick their own schools, regardless of location, and should not be inhibited by the luck or misfortune of being born in a specific location. The freedom of movement in the realm of education would be compounded with the ULT's effects on the densification of cities and towns. Schools run by companies, industry, and Sectoral Banks must also be factored into a country's educational planning to ensure high levels of employment and labor market flexibility.

Summer holidays for students (up to the age of 18) would be replaced with a form of national service (e.g., forest protection, litter cleaning) in different parts of the country from their own. Each summer students could explore new locations across their country, and associate with people of different social or cultural backgrounds who are part of the country's social fabric. This would further boost the sense of physical and social mobility, a core New Physiocratic value. It would also serve to improve physical strength, and instill a sense of national unity. The final year would culminate in a challenging, but brief, military training course, which would act as a rite of passage into adulthood.

Scale & Efficiency versus Diversity & Safety

There is a certain battle that has long been waged, with the participants of scale and efficiency on one side, and diversity and safety on another. With regards to the size of countries, trade blocs, companies, or other administrative bodies, a larger size allows for increased scale and efficiency of the economic participants; but only up to a point. At the same time, it can promote specialization over diversity, whether it be economic or cultural. The value of preserving and promoting cultures, as well as economic diversity, is the same as it is promoting diversity in farm crops. An unexpected event might wipe out a monoculture, but might also trigger tremendous growth within a few specific species. Large, keystone banks are too big to fail without causing systemic collapse, while those that are too small may fail to reap the benefits of scale. In the same way, economies and cultures must be prepared for unknown and unexpected shocks, and must be ready for unknown and unexpected opportunities.

To ensure adequate scale is achieved, without risking the loss of economic or cultural diversity, a measure of unity should be obtained between countries or regions that are already culturally and economically similar. In many cases this would mean neighnbours (e.g., Russia and Central Asian countries), but in other cases this might be places with a shared history and language, such as the UK, Canada, Australia, and some of the Caribbean nations. Some nations may already be large or populated enough to stand alone and still have the advantages of both scale and security, while smaller nations have a multitude of other considerations. Yet some small nations, such as Singapore, do manage to retain a degree of economic diversity and (not coincidentally) utilize some principles of the New Physiocracy. Innovation is required when trying to achieve this desired balance. For example with agriculture in such small states, innovations such as vertical farming might prove key in the future to attaining more security and self-reliance. The key lesson is that balance is vital in this debate, keeping in mind the advantages of both scale and diversity.

Within countries themselves, regional cultures and lifestyles must be preserved, but within the context of national unity. This might require national, in addition to regional branding. Multiregional countries must be defined and branded as an amalgamation of these regions, granting them autonomy but not independence. Maintaining the balance between scale and diversity might require abolishing provinces and municipalities, in favor of governing units inside countries that are sized somewhere in between the two. This would also abolish a layer of bureaucracy and increase the advantages of scale for cities and towns, yet allow for more policy experimentation and innovation by these governing units. It would also weaken breakaway regions' drives for independence through statehood, by creating greater rifts and discourse within them.

The most pressing economic issues of the past decade within this debate on scale have been with regards to national and global financial systems. The question must be asked about when the advantages of scale are outweighed by an institution becoming too big to fail. While large financial institutions may have more stability within themselves due to a greater range of assets, they also create a system being supported atop fewer and fewer pillars. While positive data might point to short-term stability, unexpected shock would cause systemic collapse. Furthermore, lack of competition in the financial sector limits selection and raises costs for startup funding, while large institutions show disinterest in small business, creating opportunity for oligopolies to arise in other economic sectors too. Financial regulatory agencies must include a mandate to limit size beyond the point of scale advantages, aided by a complete separation of commercial and investment banking and restrictions on domestic and foreign takeovers in the financial sector. Similar issues can also occur in other economic spheres, creating towns reliant on single companies, lack of choice for both consumers and labor, and reduced purchasing power. With the COT parliamentary chamber mandated with streamlining regulation and eradicating corruption, these goals are completely institutionalized, and the opportunities for patronage and monopolistic behavior can be purged. By granting startups a permanent voice and entrenching their interests in the system (in the case of the Startup Bank), a constant stream of new competition and innovation can finally emerge and flourish.

Wasted Legal Efforts

The war on drugs has failed in every possible way, and in every possible place. Even countries with strict, devout, religious regimes in the Middle

East and Central Asia have battled with drug addiction. An immeasurable number of resources have been spent fighting drugs and the crime issues that accompany them, yet they do not work. While governments should not condone hard drug use, or any substance abuse, they should acknowledge what works and what doesn't. The decriminalization and legalization measures that have been implemented in some countries have shown to be a success with lower rates of drug abuse, addiction, and harm. Legalization with regulation and taxation is the only way to eliminate drug cartels, drug crimes, and government waste. Tax and license revenues should go directly to health care and addiction centers, so as not to produce perverse incentives for governments to cash out on this behavior. Soft drugs (such as alcohol and marijuana) must be sold in specially licensed shops, with special consumption taxes on these products used to fund health care for the general population. Perhaps it should be considered that harder drugs should be available for sale in addiction treatment centers (after a consultation) to wean users off drugs and direct away from funding organized crime, under a similar tax regime. Drug users should pay the public instead of criminal gangs, and the public should not foot the bill for the crimes of gangs and addicts. Consumers should be informed about risks, but should have the liberty to consume what they wish, as long as the public is compensated for this behavior.

Prostitution is another activity that cannot be prevented by law enforcement, and is morally agreeable between consenting adults. Sex is also an activity necessary for mental health, with therapeutic benefits, and should be accessible to all. The issues once again lie with the involvement of organized crime, the potential for physical harm, and its effects on communities. So-called "red light districts" use public space in a way that may be considered undesirable. Therefore, a few competing, government-licensed digital platforms must be created where such transactions can take place. Platform requirements should be decided by (elected) representatives of sex workers themselves, so that they have absolute control over their safety and well-being. The platforms would act as an escrow to ensure both parties are appeased (as well as the use of ratings), guaranteeing that VAT is paid, and the use of digital (versus physical) transactions would reduce danger to both worker and client. Workers would also undergo legally mandated health checks, to prevent the spread of disease, as conditions for their licenses. These privately owned, licensed platforms would also be incentivized to ensure a black market does not merge, as they would be collecting fees on the transactions for a profit.

Eliminating these black markets means less financial burden on citizens and businesses, more personal freedom, safety for the people involved, and a contribution to economic growth. It would also free up a vast amount of resources for governments to focus on more pressing issues.

A New Metric for Success

While we acknowledge the usefulness of traditional metrics such as GDP, GDP per capita, and productivity, a Physiocratic government would introduce a far more comprehensive measure for success, referred to as the Progress Index. It might be taken into consideration when designing policymakers' compensation. Each of the following indicators would be included, with different weightings (pts):

- Real median hourly income growth, adjusted for purchasing power of essentials* — 10 pts
- Unemployment/underemployment — 7 pts
- Labor force participation — 7 pts
- Productivity growth rate (GDP per hour worked) — 7 pts
- Leisure time (inverse of hours worked per year) — 7 pts
- Total fertility rate, proximity to 2.5 children per mother — 6 pts
- Air quality — 6 pts
- Water quality and availability — 5 pts
- Health indicators — 5 pts
- Current account balance — 5 pts
- Fiscal surplus — 5 pts
- Median commute times — 5 pts
- Use of national/regional architecture (% of constructed buildings/ infrastructure) — 5 pts
- Survey on country beautification ratings — 5 pts
- Survey on availability of culture and national/regional cuisine — 5 pts
- Survey on government corruption — 5 pts
- Survey on quality of public services — 5 pts

* Purchasing power of essentials would factor in cost of living space per square meter. All indicators that comprise the Progress Index should be based on their annual rate of change.

The Progress Index measures economic growth in a way that accounts for New Physiocratic priorities; measurements which are actually felt by the population. It includes metrics to monitor changes in physical space (environmental quality and architecture), time (leisure time and commute times), and comprehensive measures of purchasing power. Finally, it ensures that unlike with simple GDP growth figures, the numbers cannot be distorted by boosting the population or inducing artificial lending booms.

Part V: The Constitution — The General Agreement

The Physiocratic constitution is what we refer to as The General Agreement. It's an agreement between all the stakeholders in society and the economy, to provide an exceptionally high standard of living for the population, including adequate living space and leisure time. In return, the population grants all stakeholders a space to share their opinions, ideas and concerns, as well as a world-class environment to conduct commerce (in a manner that's healthy for all citizens). Under the General Agreement, all the components of government and society agree to work toward the long-term interests of the country and its citizenry.

A Physiocratic constitution would guarantee citizens the right to time and space; ample physical space for their own needs (living, business), as well as plenty of free time to pursue their own creative desires outside of their place of employment. It would guarantee this without uncompensated intrusion (e.g., space that is visually desirable, and free time in which you cannot be reached by your employer). It would guarantee the right to a clean environment. It would guarantee the right to a life without burdensome taxation on their labor, efforts, and land improvements. It would guarantee civic freedoms, freedom of speech, privacy, and private property. It would guarantee an economy based on merit, ensuring equal opportunity rather than outcomes, and without any employment quotas. It would guarantee the right to a government free of corruption. It would guarantee rights to information. It would guarantee concerted efforts by representatives to minimize prices of Basic Essentials. Finally, it would guarantee the right to short-term employment when there is none available privately.

A separate set of rights would be guaranteed for business and entrepreneurs, including the right to have a business registered and legal to operate in less than 24 hours, and strong protections for private property. It would also guarantee the right to protection against government interference outside the law, with fair enforcement and an independent judiciary.

The New Physiocratic Platform

Economic Reform:

- A shift away from taxes on earned incomes, towards taxes on unearned incomes (land, environment, and negative externalities)
- Return our income tax and magnify our wages through the introduction of a National Income Supplement, which is part of the New Physiocrats "Three Pillars" programs
- Extend the National Income Supplement to include homemakers and the short term unemployed
- Return corporate tax revenues back to business via Sectoral Banks, an automatic mechanism in the New Physiocratic economy
- Return Capital Gains tax back to the markets through Assisted Savings Program (ASP) accounts
- Replace state pensions with ASP accounts (one of the Three Pillars), to magnify people's savings and investments
- Give all citizen-residents a share in the nation's prosperity through a National Dividend (one of the Three Pillars)
- Replace minimum wage laws with the New Physiocrats' Three Pillars programs of direct cash transfers
- Replace an overregulated labor market with maximum flexibility, training, and income security
- Implementation of a Unified Location Tax (ULT) to encourage rapid development with a focus on Basic Essentials and stunning architecture
- Employ powerful incentives to encourage long-term thinking throughout the economy and government
- Introduction of new management incentives to guarantee fair pay from employers
- Democratization of physical and visual space
- Entrench rights to private property and earned income
- Introduce permanent institutions to lead a substantial effort to increase people's purchasing power, by driving down the cost of Basic Essentials
- Achieve self-reliance and broad economic diversification, with the use of Sectoral Banks to channel the necessary funds
- Constitutional fiscal rules on spending and deficits, to minimize public debt and corrupt spending during election periods

- Introduce a constitutional government taxation and spending cap at a percentage of GDP, not including taxes/transfers from the Three Pillars program
- Introduce constitutional limits on state ownership, direct intervention, and bailouts; ensure it's consigned to the initial phase of introducing the New Physiocratic platform
- Employ a program to maximize the dispersal of labor market information, such as wages and job availability
- Mandate that industry sectors, under Sectoral Banks, each have their own training programs which ensure employment
- Create an employer of last resort, to provide temporary employment in public works when all else fails
- Tax short term capital inflows, with the revenues funding ASP accounts and Sectoral Banks
- Introduce a bill of rights for business, including maximum time limit on registering a business, and protections for private property and against injustice
- Replace both protectionism and unfair trade practices with the New Physiocrats' Compensatism
- Eliminate planned obsolescence through packaging information, tax incentives, and introducing ratings and awards for durability
- Far-reaching monetary reform to prevent unsustainable debt levels
- Grant the central bank with a wider array of monetary tools, accompanied by more metrics to target
- Protect central bank independence allowing it to meet its new targets without political interference
- Introduce a 30-hour work week, with an official effort to maximize the population's free time
- Combine the reduced working hours with more flexibility on working times
- Streamline bankruptcy courts and cap wait times for cases
- Introduce the South Korean model of net neutrality and network infrastructure
- Enhance urban density through the ULT
- Prioritize smart grids and cutting edge infrastructure, with targets to minimize commute times and maximize free time for the population

- Limits and targets on regulatory and compliance costs for small business, included in the bill of rights for business
- Introduce targets to maximize the dispersal of information to ensure a functioning market

Political Reform:

- Introduce the most comprehensive and effective crackdown on corruption and waste in history, and create permanent institutions to solidify the progress
- Tremendous simplification of bureaucracy and introduction of e-governance to replace the vast majority of paperwork
- Practice the utilization of policies based on empirical evidence, adapting governance policies from other nations achieving the best results
- Give official weight in government institutions to the importance of visual space, particularly architecture
- Change to a quadriacameral legislature, which acts as a forum for individuals, economic sectors, and societal sectors to work together to meet the nation's goals
- Ensure that the interests of long-term thinking and elimination of corruption and waste have significant representation in parliament
- Enshrine the independence of the judiciary into the constitution

Social Reform:

- Official policy to respect and learn from history and tradition
- Complete legalization, regulation, and taxation of drugs and prostitution
- Publicly funded schools with vouchers, where students can choose their school instead of being tied to one district
- Replace summer holidays in schools with a form of national service to gain a sense of exploration as well as locational and social mobility
- Recognize the role of marriage in the current age demographic crisis
- Comprehensive marriage reform to ensure a more lasting union, and with fairness and justice being a top priority

- Recognize the valuable role of those who choose to raise children at home, and expanding the National Income Supplement to them
- Constitutional respect for free speech, expanding it to all public property including universities/education facilities
- Compensation for infringements on privacy; a tax on big data to contribute to the national dividend
- Immigration policy focused on bringing in those who are needed and desired, rather than clouded by age demographic needs
- Introduce a New Physiocratic "Progress Index" as a new principal metric for success, alongside usual GDP and unemployment measures

Revenue Source	Rate	Revenue Destination	Details
Unified Location Tax			
Land Value Tax	3%	National and Local governments	Tax on land value — with up to 50% deduction for construction materials and agricultural inputs.
Land Size Tax	1%	National and Local governments	Tax on land value multiplied by land size to encourage urban density.
Property Externality Tax	0-0.5%	National Dividend	Tax on properties not meeting architectural or environmental guidelines.
Luxury Property Tax	0-0.5%	National Dividend	Tax on properties not providing affordable housing (defined as a % of median income).
Vacant Land Tax	1%	National and Local governments	Tax on vacant land (does not include forests or protected lands).
Sustainable VAT	24%	16% VAT to National and Local governments + 4% VAT for National Income Supplement + 4% to Sectoral Banks	Exemptions for fresh domestic food, National Eateries, property and reduced (12%) rate for recycled goods, and repairs. In addition to providing general government revenues, it will help capture income gains for the NIS, and direct increases in consumption to also increase production (via Sectoral Banks), negating inflationary pressures.

Luxury Tax (VAT)	32%	National Income Supplement	VAT rate on the top 20 goods/services purchased exclusively by the top income bracket.
Income Tax	8-24%	National Income Supplement	Income tax rates are deeply negative when factoring in the income supplement. Tax brackets are based on income percentiles, not on absolute values.
Corporate Tax	8%	Sectoral Banks	Effective corporate tax rates approach zero or negative rates after Sectoral Bank Transfers Sectoral banks are exempt from this tax.
Executive Inequality Tax — Individuals	32%	National Income Supplement	Top tax bracket for executive incomes earned in excess of a certain multiple of lowest earning (percentile) employees/contractors.
Executive Inequality Tax — Corporate	0-2%	National Income Supplement	Surtax on firms affected by the Executive Inequality Tax, ensures shareholders are incentivized to maintain wage fairness.
Monopolies — Special Rate	24%	National Dividend	Tax on private natural monopolies (e.g., power or gas distribution).
Financial Institutions — Special Rate	24%	1/2 to Sectoral Banks 1/4 to National Dividend 1/4 to National Income Supplement	A special corporate tax rate on financial institutions to compensate for licensing privileges, and to manage private debt. Sectoral banks are exempt from this tax.
Corporate Non-Integration Tax	0-2%	Sectoral Banks	Surtax on firms without cash holdings, R&D, stock listing, management or significant operations located domestically. Rate varies depending on how many criteria are met. Prevents firms from using the country as a tax haven, or a branch-plant economy.
Capital Gains Tax	4-24%	ASP Accounts	Excludes property. Rates are based on total income and length of time holding the asset. Uses 8-16-24% rate (based on income), but rate is cut in [up to] half (prorated) on 0-5 years of holding the asset. All revenues are returned to the market by distributing to people's ASP Accounts.

High Frequency Capital Gains Tax	32%	ASP Accounts	Special tax rate on capital gains on trades conducted within 10 seconds of each other. Retail clients would benefit from these trades they are unable to make, as revenues move to their investment accounts.
Dividend Tax	24%	ASP Accounts	Dividends that are not reinvested (long-term) would be taxed at the top income tax rate.
Pollutant Tax	TBD	Electrical Energy Bank	Tax on pollutants, carbon, methane, and other greenhouse gases.
Private Seigniorage Tax	0.3%	1/3 to Sectoral Banks 1/3 to National Dividend 1/3 to National and Local governments	Based on the UK's Bank Levy, a tax on total bank (and credit institution) debts. Compensates for inflationary pressures of monetary growth, and for privileged use of the monetary system. More lending would better translate into higher incomes (National Dividend), higher supply/lower prices for Basic Essentials (via Sectoral Bank funding), and greater public investment.
Trade Tariffs	TBD	Sectoral Banks of affected sectors (Sectoral Banks)	Import/export trade tariff revenues would be channeled to the affected sectors via the Sectoral Banks.
Fisheries Tax	TBD	Sustainable Aquaculture — Agriculture Bank	Transfers resources from fishing in public waters to sustainable fish farms.
Public Passages Tax	TBD	National Dividend	A tax on waterways, airports, and airwaves to compensate the public for use of public passageways.
Unutilized Patents Tax	TBD	National Dividend	A tax on patent trolls to compensate for withholding intellectual property development.
Big Data Tax	TBD	National Dividend	Compensates the public for use of their personal data.
Pigovian / Health (tobacco, drugs, sugar)	TBD	Health care	Funds health care while reducing externalities of poor health choices.

Resources Extraction Tax	TBD	1/6th to National Dividend 1/6th to National Income Supplement 1/3rd to Sectoral Banks 1/3rd to Sovereign Wealth Fund	In lieu of land taxes (which would force rapid depletion of resources) for mineral extraction, oil, and gas firms.
Speculative Inflows Tax	0-12%	1/2 to Long Term Investment Accounts 1/2 to Sectoral Banks	A tax on short-term capital inflows, based on the Chilean model. Rate is prorated for the amount of time invested up to 5 years.
Media Provider Tax	8%	Cultural Bank	Small surtax on private media profits to fund public media and domestic cultural projects.
Gas Tax	TBD	Infrastructure Bank	Gasoline tax to help fund infrastructure projects.
Monetary Financing	TBD	As determined by the central bank	Possibility of monetary financing for consumption support, employment, or public/private investment. To be determined by the completely independent central bank, strictly in pursuit of its mandates.
Sectoral Bank Tax	2%*	Evenly across Sectoral Banks	Cash/liquid assets held by Sectoral Banks would be taxed and redistributed evenly across all the Sectoral Banks. This would ensure that resources are utilized, and any excess is redistributed to the sectors which most need them.

The Road to Power

With a comprehensive platform, a symbol, a flag, and a complete vision of a New Physiocratic future, we can unite like-minded individuals and political parties around the globe. This book not only provides the framework for a New Physiocratic government, but it also aims to act as the criteria for our certification body, to ensure that the values of this movement are held to strict standards. The movement will grow, and no longer will individuals be divided by politics, but will instead be united by a common dream of how we envision our communities, our countries, and our world. Through good policy, we can take back our earned income, democratize our use of space, return to an era of beautiful architecture and durable goods, and regain our lost time.

Glossary

This glossary presents terms that we introduced to form the New Physiocratic lexicon.

ULT — A combined land and property tax, more heavily weighted towards taxing land. By taxing all land, but taxing only buildings that don't meet particular criteria, it is engineered to rationally raise government revenue, democratize physical space, and spur types of development that are beneficial to the population, without the need for zoning regulations.

Three Pillars — A system that refers to the combined National Dividend, National Income Supplement, and Assisted Savings Program. It returns tax revenues back to labor and capital; dramatically boosting incomes, savings, and investment through direct cash transfers.

ND — The National Dividend, a monthly payment made to all adult citizen-residents of the country, regardless of employment status. All recipients would receive the same amount. The amount would not be fixed, as it would be divided from the pool of revenues collected from its mandated sources, specifically those classified as the commons (aside from land).

NIS — The National Income Supplement, a monthly payment made to citizen-residents in the labor force, including homemakers. Workers would receive this as part of their salary. Those earning the average (mean) income or more would receive the full amount, as would homemakers with children. Those earning less than the average income would receive a prorated amount relative to their income. The amount would not be fixed, as it would be divided from the pool of revenues collected from its mandated sources. The funds for the NIS would include the entirety of personal income tax revenues and a portion of the VAT, to capture a portion of income gains across all income brackets.

This would ensure that each income bracket benefits from one another's successes, as the ASP payment would grow or shrink depending on the size of the revenue pool.

ASP — The Assisted Savings Program, a payment made into an [ASP] account for savings and investments, which all adult citizen-residents would hold. The payment delivered to these accounts would be based on how much an individual contributes, and would be divided from the pool of revenues collected from its mandated sources, including all capital gains tax revenues.

Basic Essentials — The essentials for living, including food, water, housing, clothing, security, electricity, and all the materials/components to produce them.

Static Sectors — Related to Basic Essentials, this refers to economic sectors that maintain a floor on the demand for their products, because their production is related to the essentials for survival.

Dynamic Sectors — This refers to economic sectors which change rapidly because they are on the cutting edge, particularly in technology. These sectors typically produce internationally competitive high value goods and services, but are likely to face disruptions in the face of rapidly changing market conditions.

Traditional Sectors — This refers to economic sectors which pertain to culture and tradition, particular artisan and cottage industries.

Sectoral Banks — These are the 16 banks which would be represented and owned by different industry sectors, with specific mandates to meet economic objectives, and which act as a mechanism to return corporate tax revenues back to business.

SVAT — A Sustainable Value-Added-Tax; a VAT (tax on consumption — goods & services) with sustainability objectives, in addition to being a main source of government revenue.

Progress Index — An index used to measure a country's success beyond simple measures such as GDP.

Compensatism — A trade policy that is an alternative to both protectionism and free trade, which instead compensates for unfairness in trade due to artificial market distortions, location of natural resources, and the stranglehold of incumbents on a world market.

Sovereign Wealth Fund — A government investment fund to hold surplus fiscal revenues, modeled on similar funds used by other countries.

Annex I

By Economist Josh Ryan-Collins, published in "Evonomics":
evonomics.com/josh-ryan-collins-land-economic-theory/

How Land Disappeared from Economic Theory

For classical economists, it was a factor of production, and the source of "rent."
Anyone who has studied economics will be familiar with the "factors of production." The best known are 'capital' (machinery, tools, computers) and 'labor' (physical effort, knowledge, skills). The standard neo-classical production function is a combination of these two, with capital typically substituting for labor as firms maximize their productivity via technological innovation. The theory of marginal productivity argues that under certain assumptions, including perfect competition, market equilibrium will be attained when the marginal cost of an additional unit of capital or labor is equal to its marginal revenue. The theory has been the subject of considerable controversy, with long debates on what is really meant by capital, the role of interest rates and whether it is neatly substitutable with labor.

But there has always been a third 'factor': Land. Neglected, obfuscated but never quite completely forgotten, the story of Land's marginalization from mainstream economic theory is little known. But it has important implications. Putting it back into economics, we argue in a new book, *Rethinking the Economics of Land and Housing*, could help us better understand many of today's most pressing social and economic problems, including excessive property prices, rising wealth inequality and stagnant productivity. Land was initially a key part of classical economic theory, so why did it get pushed aside?

Classical economics, land and economic rent
The classical political economists — David Ricardo, John Stuart Mill, and Adam Smith — who shaped the birth of modern economics,

emphasized that land had unique qualities, distinct from capital and labor, which had important influence on the dynamics of production.

They recognized that land was inherently fixed and scarce. Ricardo's concept of 'economic rent' referred to the gains accruing to landholders from their exclusive ownership of a scarce resource: desirable agricultural land. Ricardo argued that the landowner was not free to choose the economic rent he or she could charge. Rather, it was determined by the cost to the laborer of farming the next most desirable but un-owned plot. Rent was thus driven by the marginal productivity of land, not labor as the population theorist Thomas Malthus had argued. On the flip side, as Adam Smith (1776: 162) noted, neither did land rents reflect the efforts of the land-owner:

"The rent of land, therefore, considered as the price paid for the use of the land, is naturally a monopoly price. It is not at all proportioned to what the landlord may have laid out upon the improvement of the land, or to what he can afford to take; but to what the farmer can afford to give."

The classical economists feared that landowners would increasingly monopolise the proceeds of growth as nations developed and desirably locational land became relatively scarcer. Eventually, as rents rose, the proportion of profits available for capital investment and wages would become so small as to lead to economic stagnation, inequality and rising unemployment. In other words, economic rent could crowd out productive investment.

Marxist and socialist thinkers proposed to deal with the problem of rent by nationalizing and socializing land, in other words, destroying the institution of private property. But the classical economists had a strong attachment to the latter, seeing it as a bulwark of liberal democracy and encouraging of economic progress. They instead proposed to tax it. Indeed, they argued that the majority of taxation of the nation should come from increases in land values that would naturally occur in a developing economy. Mill (1884: 629-630) saw taxation of land as a natural extension of private property:

"In such a case ...[land rent]... it would be no violation of the principles on which private property is grounded, if the state should appropriate this increase of wealth, or part of it, as it arises. This would not properly be taking anything from anybody; it would merely be applying an accession of wealth, created by circumstances, to the benefit of society, instead of allowing it to become an unearned appendage to the riches of a particular class."

Ricardo and Smith were mainly writing about an agrarian economy. But the law of rent applies equally in developed urban areas as the famous Land Value Tax campaigner Henry George argued in his best-selling text 'Progress and Poverty.' Once all the un-owned land is occupied, economic rent then becomes determined by *locational* value. Thus the rise of communications technology and globalization has not meant 'the end of distance' as some predicted. Instead, it has driven the economic pre-eminence of a few cities that are best connected to the global economy and offer the best amenities for the knowledge workers and entrepreneurs of the digital economy. The scarcity of these locations has fed a long boom in the value of land in those cities.

Neoclassical economics and the obfuscation of land

The classical economists were 'political' in the sense that they saw a key role for the state and in particular taxation in preventing the institution of private property from constraining economic development via rent. But at the turn of the nineteenth century, a group of economists began to develop a new kind of economics, based upon universal scientific laws of supply and demand, and free of normative judgements concerning power and state intervention. Land's uniqueness as an input to production was lost along the way.

John Bates Clark was one of the leading American economists of the time and was recognised as the founder of neoclassical capital theory. He argued that Ricardo's law of rent generated from the marginal productivity of land applied equally to capital and labor. It mattered little what the intrinsic properties of the factors of production were and it was better to consider them "... as business men conceive of it, abstractly, as a sum or fund of value in productive uses ... the earnings of these funds constitute in each case a differential gain like the product of land." (Bates Clark 1891: 144-145)

Clark developed the notion of an all-encompassing "fund" of "pure capital" that is homogeneous across land, labor and capital goods. From this rather fuzzy concept, developed marginal productivity theory. Land still exists in the short-run in this approach — and indeed in microeconomics textbooks — when it is generally assumed that some factors may be fixed. For example, you cannot immediately build a new factory or develop a new product to respond to new demands or changes in technology. But in the long run — which is what counts when thinking about equilibrium — all factors of production will be subject to the same variable marginal returns. All factors can be reduced to equivalent physical quantities; if a firm adds an additional unit of labor, capital goods or land to its production process, it will be homogeneous to all previous units.

Early 20th Century English and American economists adopted and developed Clark's theory into a comprehensive theory of distribution of income and economic growth that eventually usurped political economy approaches. Clark's work became the basis for the seminal neoclassical 'two-factor' growth models of the 1930s developed by Roy Harrod and Bob Solow. Land — defined as locational space — is absent from such macroeconomic models.

The reasons for this may well be political. Mason Gaffney, an American land economist and scholar of Henry George, has argued that Bates Clark and his followers received substantial financial support from corporate and landed interests who were determined to prevent George's theories gaining credibility out of concerns that their wealth would be whittled away via a land tax. In contrast, theories of land rent and taxation never found an academic home. In addition, George, primarily a campaigner and journalist, never managed to forge an allegiance with American socialists who were more focused on taxing the profits of the captains of industry and the financial sector.

The result was the burden of taxation came to fall upon capital (corporation tax) and labor (income tax) rather than land. A final factor preventing theories of land rent from taking off in the U.S. may have been the simple fact that at the beginning of the 20th century, land scarcity and fixity were perhaps less a political issue in the still expanding U.S. than in Europe, where a land value tax came closer to being adopted.

Why land is different
At first glance, neoclassical economics' conflation of land with a broad notion of capital does seem to follow a certain logic. It is clear that both

can be thought of as commodities: both can be bought and sold in a mature capitalist market. A firm can have a portfolio of assets that includes land (or property) and shares in a company (the equivalent of owning capital 'stock') and swap one for another using established market prices. Both land and capital goods can also be seen as stores of value (consider the phrase 'safe as houses') and to some extent a source of liquidity, particularly given innovations in finance that have allowed people to engage in home equity withdrawal.

In reality, however, land and capital are fundamentally distinctive phenomena. Land is permanent, cannot be produced or reproduced, cannot be 'used up' and does not depreciate. None of these features apply to capital. Capital goods are produced by humans, depreciate over time due to physical wear and tear and innovations in technology (think of computers or mobile phones), and they can be replicated. In any set of national accounts, you will find a sizeable negative number detailing physical capital stock 'depreciation': *net* not *gross* capital investment is the preferred variable used in calculating a nation's output. When it comes to land, net and gross values are equal.

The argument made by Bates Clark and his followers was that by removing the complexities of dynamics, the true or pure functioning of the economy will be more clearly revealed. As a result, microeconomic theory generally deals with relations of coexistence or 'comparative statics' (how labor and capital are combined in a single point in time to create outputs) rather than dynamic relations. This has led to a neglect of the continued creation and destruction of capital and the continued existence and non-depreciation of land.

Indeed, although land values change with — or some would say drive — economic and financial cycles, in the long run land value usually *appreciates* rather than depreciates like capital. This is inevitable when you think about it — as the population grows, the economy develops and the capital stock increases, land remains fixed. The result is that land values (ground rents) must rise, unless there is some countervailing non-market intervention.

Indeed, there is good argument that as economies mature, the demand for land relative to other consumer goods increases. Land is a 'positional good', the desire for which is related to one's position in society *vis a vis* others and thus not subject to diminishing marginal returns like other factors. As technological developments drive down the costs of other goods, so competition over the most prized locational space rises and eats up a greater and greater share of people's income as Adair Turner has recently argued. A recent study of 14 advanced economies found that 81% of house price increases between 1950 and 2012 can be explained by rising land prices with the remainder attributable to increases in construction costs

Consequences of the neglect of land

Today's economics textbooks — in particular microeconomics — slavishly follow the tenets of marginal productivity theory. 'Income' is understood narrowly as a reward for one's contribution to production whilst wealth is understood as 'savings' due to one's productive investment effort, not as unearned windfalls from being the owner of land or other naturally scarce sources of value. In many advanced economies land values — and capital gains made from increasing property prices — are not properly measured and tracked over time. As Steve Roth has noted for *Evonomics*, the U.S.' National accounts do not properly take into account capital gains and changes in household's 'net worth,' much of which is driven by changes in land values.

Even progressive economists such as Thomas Piketty have fallen into this trap. Once you strip out capital gains (mainly on housing), Piketty's spectacular rise in the wealth-to-income ratio recorded in advanced economics in the last 30 years starts to look very ordinary (Figure 1 shows the comparison for great Britain since 1970).

In the UK, land is not included as a distinct asset class in the National Accounts, despite being one of the largest and most important asset classes in the economy. Instead, the value of the underlying land is included in the value of dwellings and other buildings and structures, which are classed as 'produced non-financial assets' (Figure 2)

As shown in Figure 2, the value of 'dwellings' (homes and the land underneath them) has increased by four times (or 400%) between 1995 and 2015, from £1.2 trillion to £5.5 trillion, largely due to increases in house prices rather than a change in the volume of dwellings. In contrast the forms of 'capital' that we associate with increases in wealth and productivity — commercial buildings, machinery, transport, Information and communications technology have grown much more slowly.

Thus this huge growth in wealth relative to the rest of the economy originates not from the saving of income derived from people's

Figure 1: Piketty's Wealth to income ratio including and excluding capital gains (Great Britain, 1970–2010)

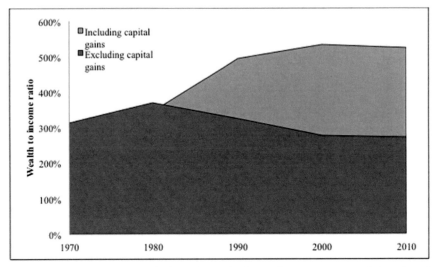

Source: Ryan-Collins et al. (2017) *Rethinking the Economics of Land and Housing,* Zed Books: London, p.172. Credit: Evonomics/ evonomics.com/ josh-ryan-collins-land-economic-theory/

Figure 2: Growth in the value of non-financial assets in the UK, 1995–2015

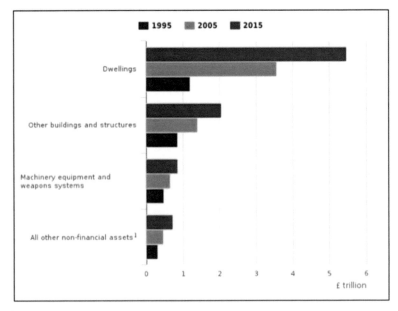

Credit: ONS

contribution to production (activity that would have created jobs and raised incomes), but rather from windfalls resulting from exclusive control of a scarce natural resource: land.

This may help us explain — at least in part — the great 'productivity puzzle' — that is, why productivity (and related average incomes) has been flat-lining, even as 'wealth' has been increasing. The puzzle is explained by the fact that the majority of the growth in wealth has come from capital gains rather than increased profits (or savings) derived from productive investment. Savings are at a 50-year low in the UK even as the wealth to income ratio hits record highs.

When the value of land under a house goes up, the total productive capacity of the economy is unchanged or diminished because nothing new has been produced: it merely constitutes an increase in the value of the asset. This may increase the wealth of the landowner and they may choose to spend more or draw down some of that wealth via home equity withdrawal. But they equally may not. Moreover, the rise in the value of that asset has a corresponding cost: someone else in the economy will have to save more for a deposit or see their rents increase and as a result spend less (or, in the case of the firm, invest less).

In current national accounts, however, only the increase in wealth is recorded, whilst the present discounted value of the decreased flow of resources to the rest of the economy is ignored as Joe Stiglitz has pointed out. Rising land values suck purchasing power and demand out of the economy, as the benefits of growth are concentrated in property owners with a low marginal propensity to consume, which in turn reduces spending and investment. In addition, most new credit creation by the banking system now flows into real estate rather than productive activity. This crowds out productive investment, both by the banking system itself and non-bank investors who see the potential for much higher returns on relatively tax free real estate investment.

Land values also fundamentally affect the impact of monetary policy, particularly in financially liberalized economies. If a central bank lowers interest rates to try and stimulate capital investment and consumption, it is likely to simultaneously drive up land prices and the economic rent attached to them as more credit flows into the mortgages for domestic and commercial real estate. This has a naturally perverse effect on the capital investment and consumption effects that the lowering of interest rates was intended to achieve.

But for mainstream economists and policy makers these connections between the value of land and the macroeconomy are ignored. Housing demand is assumed to be subject to the same rules that drive desire for any other commodity: its marginal productivity and utility. Rising house prices or rents (relative to incomes) — an urgent problem in countries such as the United Kingdom — can be attributed to insufficient supply of homes or land. As with other policy challenges, such as unemployment, the focus is on the supply side. The distribution of land and property wealth across the population, its taxation and the role of the banking system in driving up prices through increases in mortgage debt are neglected. Planning rules and other easy targets such as immigration are then blamed for the loss of control people feel as a result of insecure housing rather than its true structural causes in the land economy.

Land rents: there is a "free lunch"
Although presented as an objective theory of distribution, in fact marginal productivity theory has a strong normative element. Ultimately it leads us to a world, where, so long as there is sufficient competition and free markets, all will receive their just deserts in relation to their true contribution to society. There will, in Milton Friedman's famous terms, be "no such thing as a free lunch."

But marginal productivity theory says nothing about the *distribution* of the ownership of factors of production — not least land. Landed-property is implicitly assumed to be the most efficient organisational form for enabling private exchange and free markets with little questioning of how property and tenure rights are distributed nor of the gains (rents) that possession of such rights grants to its holders. Ultimately, this limits what the theory can say about the distribution of income, particularly in a world where such economic rents are large. Land is the "mother of all monopolies" as Winston Churchill once put it — and hence the most important one for economists to understand.

But if economists are to focus on land, they must get their hands dirty. They must start examining the role of institutions, including systems of land-ownership, property-rights, land taxation and mortgage credit that are historically determined by power and class relations. In fact it is these inherently political, social and cultural developments that determine the way in which economic rent is distributed and with it, macroeconomic dynamics more generally.

2017 April 4

Smith, Adam (1776) An Inquiry into the Nature and Causes of the Wealth of Nations. W. Strahan and T. Cadell.

Mill, John Stuart (1884) *Principles of Political Economy*, D. Appleton

Bates *Clark, John Bates. (1891) 'Marshall's Principles of Economics'. Political Science, Quarterly 6 (1): 126—51.*

Annex II

The following is the original Georgist constitution; from platform of the Single Tax League of the United States, adopted September 3, 1890. While the constitution of the New Physiocrats is vastly expanded upon and modernized for the current era, here we find some of its roots and core principles.

Paragraph 1
"We assert as our fundamental principle the self-evident truth enunciated In the Declaration of American Independence, that all men are created equal, and are endowed by their Creator with certain Inalienable rights."

Paragraph 2
"We hold that all men are equally entitled to the use and enjoyment of what God has created and of what is gained by the general growth and improvement of the community of which they are a part. Therefore, no one should be permitted to hold natural opportunities without a fair return to all for any special privilege thus accorded to him, and that value which the growth and improvement of the community attach to land should be taken for the use of the community."

Paragraph 3
"We hold that each man is entitled to all that his labor produces. Therefore no tax should be levied on the products of labor."

Paragraph 4
"To carry out these principles we are in favor of raising all public revenues for national, state, county and municipal purposes by a single tax upon land values, irrespective of Improvements, and of the abolition of all forms of direct and indirect taxation."

Paragraph 5
"Since in all our states we now levy some tax on the value of land, the single tax can be instituted by the simple and easy way of abolishing, one after another all other taxes now levied, and commensurately increasing the tax on land values, until we draw upon that one source for all expenses of government, the revenue being divided between local governments, state governments and the general government, as the revenue from direct taxes Is now divided between the local and state governments; or, a direct assessment being made by the general government upon the states and paid by them from revenues collected in this manner."

Paragraph 6
"The single tax we propose is not a tax on land, and therefore would not fall on the use of land and become a tax on labor."

Paragraph 7
"It is a tax, not on land, but on the value of land. Thus it would not fall on all land, but only on valuable land and on that not in proportion to the use made of it, but in proportion to its value — the premium which the user of land must pay to the owner, either in purchase money or rent, for permission to use valuable land. It would thus be a tax, not on the use or improvement of land, but on the ownership of land, taking what would otherwise go to the owner as owner, and not as user."

Paragraph 8
"In assessments under the single tax all values created by individual use or improvement would be excluded and the only value taken into consideration would be the value attaching to the bare land by reason of neighborhood, etc., to be determined by impartial periodical assessments. Thus the farmer would have no more taxes to pay than the speculator who held a similar piece of land idle, and the man who on a city lot erected a valuable building would be taxed no more than the man who held a similar lot vacant."

Paragraph 9
"The single tax, in short, would call upon men to contribute to the public revenues, not in proportion to what they produce or accumulate,

but in proportion to the value of the natural opportunities they hold. It would compel them to pay just as much for holding land idle as for putting it to its fullest use."

Paragraph 10

"The single tax, therefore, would—

Section 1
Take the weight of taxation off of the agricultural districts where land has little or no value irrespective of improvements, and put it on towns and cities where bare land rises to a value of millions of dollars per acre.

Section 2
Dispense with a multiplicity of taxes and a horde of tax gatherers, simplify government and greatly reduce its cost.

Section 3
Do away with the fraud, corruption and gross inequality inseparable from our present methods of taxation, which allow the rich to escape while they grind the poor. Land cannot be hidden or carried off and its value can be ascertained with greater ease and certainty than any other.

Section 4
Give us with all the world as perfect freedom of trade as now exists between the states of our Union, thus enabling our people to share, through free exchanges, in all the advantages which nature has given to other countries, or which the peculiar skill of other peoples has enabled them to attain. It would destroy the trusts, monopolies and corruptions which are the outgrowths of the tariff. It would do away with the fines and penalties now levied on anyone who improves a farm, erects a house, builds a machine, or in any way adds to the general stock of wealth. It would leave everyone free to apply labor or expend capital in production or exchange without fine or restriction, and would leave to each the full product of his exertion.

Section 5

It would, on the other hand, by taking for public use that value which attaches to land by reason of the growth and improvement of the community, make the holding of land unprofitable to the mere owner, and profitable only to the user. It would thus make it impossible for speculators and monopolists to hold natural opportunities unused or only half used, and would throw open to labor the illimitable field of employment which the earth offers to man. It would thus solve the labor problem, do away with involuntary poverty, raise wages in all occupations to the full earnings of labor, make overproduction impossible until all human wants are satisfied, render labor-saving inventions a blessing to all and cause such an enormous production and such an equitable distribution of wealth as would give to all comfort, leisure and participation in the advantages of an advancing civilization."

Paragraph 11

"With respect to monopolies other than the monopoly on land, we hold that where free competition becomes impossible, as in telegraphs, railroads, water and gas supplies, etc., such business becomes a proper social function, which should be controlled and managed by and for the whole people concerned, through their proper governmental, local, state or national, as may be."
— The Standard (Newspaper), October 1890

References

ACE vs. CBIT: Which is Better for Investment and Welfare? Doina Maria Radulescu Michael Stimmelmayr Ifo Institute, Munich, Center for Economic Studies, University of Munich, January 2006

Economists Explain Why Our Economy Crashes Every 18 Years, Joshua Philipp, The Epoch Times, March 25, 2016

Exclusionary zoning' is opportunity hoarding by upper middle class Richard V. Reeves, Brookings Institution, May 24, 2017

Foolish Revenge or Shrewd Regulation? Financial-Industry Tax Law Reforms Proposed in the Wake of the Financial Crisis, Richard T. Page, Georgetown University Law Center Tulane Law Review, Vol. 85, No. 191, 2010

Office for National Statistics, UK, 2017 (data on personal incomes)

Statistics Canada, 2017 (data on personal incomes)

The American Experience Of A Too High Minimum Wage: Employment Down By 35%, GDP Down By 23%, Forbes, Tim Worstall, April 24, 2016

The Revenue and Double Dividend Potential of Taxes on International Private Capital Flows and Securities Transactions, Ilene Grabel, University of Denver, February 2003 (data on revenues raised by Chilean taxes on capital inflows)

U.S. Bureau of Labor Statistics, 2017 (data on personal incomes)

Why Denser Cities Are Smarter and More Productive Richard Florida, Citylab, Dec 10, 2012